The Secrets of a Fifty-Year
Romantic Expedition

The Secrets of a Fifty-Year Romantic Expedition

A Golden Anniversary Celebration

Matthew E. McLaren, PhD

THE SECRETS OF A FIFTY-YEAR ROMANTIC EXPEDITION
A GOLDEN ANNIVERSARY CELEBRATION

Unless otherwise noted, scripture references are taken from the New King James Version (NKJV), copyright © 1982 Thomas Nelson.

iUniverse books may be ordered through booksellers or by contacting:

iUniverse
1663 Liberty Drive
Bloomington, IN 47403
www.iuniverse.com
1-800-Authors (1-800-288-4677)

ISBN: 978-1-4917-6604-0 (sc)
ISBN: 978-1-4917-6603-3 (hc)
ISBN: 978-1-4917-6602-6 (e)

Library of Congress Control Number: 2015906450

Print information available on the last page.

iUniverse rev. date: 05/30/2015

Contents

Foreword

We all have seen marriages that work well, and we've also seen some that are disasters. Historically, marriage has been a lifetime proposition. Two people, coming from differing perspectives, stood before a minister or a public official and promised that they would remain with each other until death intervened. As medical advances improved lifespan, marriages lasting fifty years or more became increasingly common. In the recent past, however, high expectations and peer pressure have led to the breakup of many marriages that began with the best intentions and great commitment. Make no mistake about it: the institution of marriage is under incredible pressure today. Relationships borne of great love and wonderful romance all too frequently settle into a dull routine that seems more like a sentence than a celebration of undying love.

Dr. Matthew McLaren has lived in the laboratory of his marriage for over fifty years. Because a laboratory is where we learn from experimenting with a variety of ideas, Dr. McLaren has made important discoveries that provide the foundation for marriages that last and that grow. Those discoveries have been gathered and placed in this book, *The Secrets of a Fifty-Year Romantic Expedition*, but also for the benefit of those of us who live in a world where marriage is truly the fundamental building block of society.

Some who are single may suspect that this book is not for them, but I think it is. No one who is about to enter into marriage should do so without a clear understanding of what the journey ahead is like. Dr. McLaren's friendly style places the foundation pillars of a lasting relationship where we can grasp them and put them into practice, right at the beginning of the relationship.

For others who have been in a marriage for a number of years, this book is a refresher, a reminder of some of the things that they've seen or experienced themselves. Even the best automobile benefits from a tune-up from time to time—and marriages are like that too. As one settles into a relationship with another person, it is easy to take for granted some parts of marriage that benefit from greater attention. This book provides that tune-up from the vantage point of one who has experience.

Throughout more than forty years of service as a church pastor and leader, I've been saddened by the broken relationships that I've witnessed all too often. Marriages begun with such hope and anticipation have failed miserably. That need not happen. What you will find in the pages that follow will provide important insight that will encourage you as you pursue the marriage of your dreams.

Mark Johnson
President
Seventh-day Adventist Church in Canada

Acknowledgments

I would like to acknowledge God for his unconditional love and blessing; Samuel and Ruby Hutton, Joy (Hutton) Harrison, and all the wonderful members of the Rollington Town Seventh-day Adventist Church for their encouragement and support given to us during our engagement and marriage preparation; and my children, grandchildren, great-grandchildren, relatives, church family, and friends for the support they have given to Theresa and me during our fifty years of marriage and family development. I am also taking the opportunity to thank the readers of this book. May the words be a blessing and inspiration to you, your marriage, and your family as you continue on this unique journey of life. Please review and provide comments. It does not matter if you agree or disagree with me; generating discussion on the subject is healthy.

To my beloved wife, this book would not be possible without you. Your commitment and unselfish love demonstrated in our marriage and family and your continuous encouragement gives me the energy and tenacity to write this book.

Introduction

The purpose of this book is to review in greater depth the marriage institution given to the first husband and wife at the beginning of creation and the value we place on marriage today. In the beginning, God created the heavens and the earth and everything in it. He created man and woman in his own image and declared that everything was very good. God performed the marriage of the first husband and wife. He gave them the precious gift of unconditional love, the biological intimate gift of making children, and dominion over the entire world and everything in it. They were trusted stewards of God's earthly kingdom. They were in constant contact with God's Law. Disobedience to God's instruction allowed the creature of deception to rob them of their Creator's priceless gifts. The first husband and wife's lack of trust in God's unconditional love caused the generations that followed to question the sacred institution of marriage. As time went by, the beginning of creation came under attack by the big bang theory revolution. God, in his infinite wisdom and unconditional love for his confused children, sent his only begotten Son to redeem his dominion and restore his moral law to his people and the sacred institution of marriage. "For God so loved the world that He gave His only begotten Son, that whoever believes in Him shall not perish, but have eternal life" (John 3:16 KJV).

I am not a marriage counselor or a psychologist. I am just a humble husband who has experienced fifty years of a challenging romantic expedition—marriage—guided and sustained by the gift of God's unconditional love. In my research on this topic, I discovered there are thousands of counselors, coaches, psychologists, and other experts who counsel married couples and offer the secrets of how to stay married. I respect the counseling of these professionals, but my personal belief and experience in God's Word, which is dispensed to us in his Holy Bible, suggests to me that there is a missing link. To sustain a successful marriage, we cannot eliminate the sacred instruction given to husband and wife at the beginning of creation. Many of the instructions that professionals give are missing the most important link—God's divine guidance. In my exploration of joyful living, every day provides new challenging and rewarding adventures. We have a lifetime to accumulate unique learning experiences that represent priceless and rare treasures. Each marriage expedition should be designed and tailored to fit the needs of each couple. I recommend that the wife and husband, who have the opportunity to travel the challenging terrains of life's journey, design an environmental health-and-safety program.

Before starting your daily activity, take time to analyze and evaluate your work and social environment for hidden physical, mental, spiritual, or emotional hazards that are threats. Take action to eliminate or contain them before they become incidents that are disruptive to your marriage and family work environment. Analyzing, eliminating, and containing hazards will allow your marriage expedition to be more productive.

Most marriages shut down because of unnecessary risk, bad planning, and lack of proper policy and procedure. It is also necessary to mentally, physically, spiritually, and emotionally prepare your mind and body for your daily tasks. Take quality time for spiritual devotion and physical and mental stretching. Your nervous system will be better balanced and react more efficiently to an emergency. Do not develop a negative attitude that will endanger your expedition.

The priceless buried treasure for which you are searching is a family environment filled with joyful experiences, such as love, contentment, peace, and serenity, established in the trust and confidence of God's benevolent blessing. These treasures can be invested to provide direction and guidance for future generations.

In the pages of this book, I will encourage wife and husband to visualize their future and paint a panoramic picture of the history they would like to leave for their children, grandchildren, and future generations. How would you like your priceless treasure to be read? Do you want future generations to be confused and disappointed by all the broken relationships and disruptive marriages and family values? Many people have asked Theresa and me what our secret is for staying married for fifty years.

The length of time we have been married is a number. It is the quality time and cooperative efforts we've shared with each other that has strengthened the foundation of our relationship. It takes love, compassion, gentleness, kindness, unselfish attitude, positive action, flexibility, endurance, responsibility, and commitment to sustain and nurture joyful living. When I retired from my bachelor lifestyle, I planned to begin a new career as a loving and caring husband, father, and provider for my family. My faith in God and my relationship with my church family, nuclear family, extended family, relatives, and friends provided a physical, mental, spiritual, and emotional foundation for us in difficult times. In my second book, *The Miracle of Love*, I gave a short description of how I met my wife. Celebrating our golden anniversary gives me the opportunity to write this book, to share our wisdom and knowledge learned from many years of challenging experiences. I hope other married couples who are planning to join us in this unique expedition will benefit from our experiences.

When Colonel Harland Sanders reached retirement age, he discovered that his pension was inadequate to sustain a comfortable lifestyle. He also realized that his experience in culinary art provided him with a unique recipe for fried chicken, which he then shared with the world as Kentucky Fried Chicken, which brought a colorful and profitable accomplishment to his senior years.

Theresa and I do not have experience in culinary art. We do have, however, fifty years of a marital recipe—kosher and seasoned with the spices of challenging experiences that we encountered in our romantic expedition. We are two loving and caring people who are willing to say thanks to God and to all the caring people whose lifestyles have motivated us and given us spiritual and moral support on our journey of life. I hope the words in this book will be viewed as a recipe for joyful living. Theresa and I will receive joyful satisfaction that will reenergize and strengthen our faith and belief in God as we continue on to our final destination.

It is said that someone asked Thomas Edison why he continued with his experiment with the light bulb after so many failures. He informed the person that he did not have failures; he discovered thousands of different ways that the filaments in the light bulb could not work. Because of his dedication and persistence, the world now experiences the success of the light bulb. As you read this book, remember that challenges in our marriages and family relationships are not failures; they are elements that will help to illuminate the pathway for a successful and joyful marriage and family lifestyle.

During our fifty-year romantic expedition, we intentionally built a marital foundation by evaluating negative factors that could cause an angry confrontation and purposefully taking action to reverse the situations. I ask myself, why did we have that argument? What can I do to prevent negative confrontation? I have learned from experience that one of the best methods to resolve conflict is to start an open discussion, such as why it is not healthy to have an argument. In an argument, no one wins. I ask myself, what did I say or do that triggered that argument? What can I do to resolve challenging conflicts? An apology, whether I think I am right or wrong, can diffuse an angry retaliation. Words can destroy, and words can heal. The Bible says, "A soft answer turns away wrath, but a harsh word stirs up anger" (Proverbs 15:1 NKJV). Never allow confrontation or disagreement to continue through a day and night. They will intensify, expand, and weaken the foundation of your relationship. Prayerfully resolve it before you go to sleep.

In our journey of life, there is always a wrong and a right pathway. If you get on the wrong pathway, you are in danger of having an incident. If you get on the wrong side, stop and think of the most efficient way to get back on the right pathway. Our journey of life provides wonderful and joyful experiences when we extend courtesy and kindness to others. Every challenging situation that is resolved strengthens the foundation of our marriage and family relationships and eliminates weakness that could cause marital pain, which could lead to sickness and death of the marriage.

I have a special message for husband, wives, and families: challenges in marriage and family life do not have to determine where your journey of life ends or the quality of life you live. Challenges are learning experiences that can be used to mold and shape your character for eternity. For Theresa and me, marriage is a unique and priceless treasure that brings wisdom, knowledge, and value to our lives. This wisdom is not learned in textbooks; it can be acquired only through years of experience with our children, relatives, friends, environment, and an intimate relationship with our Creator. I believe that if we are careless in our thinking or succumb to the oversimplification of conventional beliefs, our faith could suffer from false conception of our true potential value.

My wife and I celebrated our fiftieth wedding anniversary on February 12, 2014. I can still vividly remember the first day I saw her, the first date we had, the first time I took her into my arms, and the vow we made on our wedding day, and I can hardly realize it is fifty years since we said "I do." With great humility and pride, I take this opportunity to say that I love my first lady, my queen. With Jesus as our guiding light, we will continue to walk together until death. By the power of prayer, I found her. She is my special and rare treasure. She is a life partner with strength and compassion, a partner with integrity and goodness in her heart and actions. She has guarded the inner circle of our relationship and made it the sacred center of our lives, just for Jesus, her, and me.

God used a picture in Ezekiel 16 to describe his people. He essentially said, "When I passed by you again and looked upon you, indeed your heart was the heart of love, so I spread my arms and covered you. I went into a covenant with you, a covenant that cannot be broken." The more I know my wife, the deeper I appreciate and love her. She personifies the virtuous woman of Proverbs 31:10–31, who displays spiritual wisdom and holistic qualities that are needed for our twenty-first–century marriage and family values.

I realize Theresa may not be as perfect as I see her, but in my eyes and in my heart, there's no one else on earth more genuine and precious than she is to me, my one and only love. And there's no treasure anywhere to equal what she is worth to me. She is my lover, my friend, my sweetheart, and my wife. It has been a wonderful and challenging fifty-year journey, filled with meaningful experiences.

I have always held that glorious picture in my mind of when I saw her the first time. She was and is one of the most beautiful people in my life and is always a breath of fresh air. The radiance of her smile illuminates the darkest cloud and reflects her beauty; it softens and melts my heart. Life would never be the same without her. She is God-sent. Our first date was at the Rollington Town Seventh-day Adventist Church, when Pastor Green made the altar call. I was surprised and delighted when I walked up to the altar and she took that walk with me. In my heart, I was picturing that special walk we would take together, hand in hand, to make our second best commitment to each other, God, and the world, when we would say I do. We have accumulated wonderful treasures in our fifty-year journey. It has been a glorious blessing, and in gratitude I realize that within those fifty years, we added four of the most beautiful and wonderful children, ten grandchildren, and four great-grandchildren to our treasure chest. They are God's bountiful blessing to us and an added resource to our community and the world. The pathway was not always smooth, but we weathered the storm because we allowed Jesus into the inner circle of our marriage relationship.

I feel elated and joyful to share our experience with other married couples and families. We can leave some signposts to guide them to their destinations. As a senior married couple, I believe we have an opportunity and responsibility to encourage and motivate others to improve the foundation of their marriage and family lifestyles.

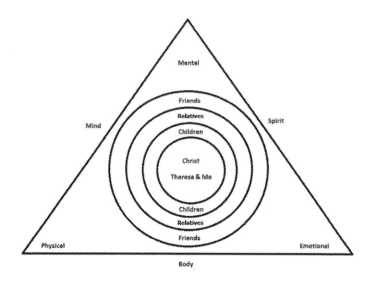

Husbands and wives should take a balanced approach to their lifestyles. They need to have balanced minds, bodies, and spirits to sustain mentally healthy and wealthy marriages and family relationships, built on the foundation of God's love, with Christ in the center of their daily activities. He will guide and help them to take control of their mental, physical, and emotional behaviors as they travel the pathway in search of joyful living.

The above triangle represents a holistic-balance foundation for a mentally, physically, and emotionally diversified environment, where family values are stored in the heart of your mind, body, and spirit. The center of the circle provides the nucleus—the oneness—where as wife and husband, you have the opportunity to allow Christ to be your pilot on your journey. Remember that you are the captain of your expedition. No one should be allowed in the control center; you are responsible for the safety of your marriage, family, and others. With Christ as your pilot, you will have the proper tools and equipment to evaluate the rugged terrain and eliminate or contain hazardous or challenging conditions before they become obstructions to your expedition.

We will cross many mountains and learn many lessons along life's journey; experience teaches me that we cannot do it alone. We need the cooperation of others who are traveling on this highway of life. We truly say thanks to God for guiding us to the highway that leads to the right destination. When the journey becomes challenging, I know that we have Jesus Christ, our friends, and our family, who are willing to use their talents—mentally, spiritually, emotionally, and physically—to help us remove dangerous threats to our marriage and family. Many people have changed direction because they could not follow the highway sign that reads "Until death do we part." The path we have taken has led to joyful living. Unconditional love is the greatest incentive to guide us on the highway of life. Love is the true character of Christ, and we are made and shaped in his image. "Then God said, 'Let Us make man in Our image, according to Our likeness …' So God created man in His own image; in the image of God He created him; male and female He created them" (Genesis 1:26–27 NKJV). When Adam and Eve sinned, God gave them a second chance by extending his *agape love* (unconditional love). Why is it that so many of us find it so difficult to give our marriages a second chance?

Marriage is a sacred vow; when we are joined together, we become one. The equation changes from one and one makes two, to two equals one. Marriage should not be taken lightly. When twins are born joined together, it takes surgery by skilled physicians to separate them, and it sometimes involves sacrificing vital parts or even the life of one twin to save the other. When wife and husband separate, there are always consequences. Some men and women have divided their accumulated material possessions and take on added responsibility, supporting two families.

When children are added to the equation, they are separated from mother or father. The mother or father may become a single parent. This could cause financial burdens and added stressors; the children could become rebellious or depressed, blaming themselves for their parents' failure.

> Whether your kids witness screaming matches between you and your husband or see you coolly treating one another with forced politeness, they know what it means. According to developmental researchers at university of California at Berkley who randomly selected couples with school age children to participate in a marital intervention, the children whose parents worked to improve their marriage through this intervention, did better in school than children of parents who did not. Your marriage is the first guideline your children have for relationship. *(Global Post 2015)*

The choice is yours. Think of your children. Let God guide you when you are making your decision and remember, grace and mercy say no.

1

Personal Experience

Life is a continuous journey, and this journey can take many detours. The actions we take and the choices we make will determine how safely we get to our destinations. We dream of things we wish to accomplish and should never give up on our goals and objectives, which are needed for comfort, relaxation, and joyful living. Our belief, faith, and action will give us confidence to achieve the success we truly deserve.

There are times when you will need to detour to avoid traffic congestion. Whenever this happens, make sure your GPS guides you back to the right highway. Every day is a new beginning with new experiences. You can reflect on your past experiences and learn from them, but it is not possible to erase the journey you traveled yesterday. Your journey through childhood can make a lasting impression on your adult life. At an early age, you do not have any control of where you travel or live, the things you eat, the clothes you wear, or the places you go.

In youth, we dream of things that we wish to accomplish. The things to which we are exposed can affect our abilities to choose the right partners, positively or negatively, as well as the pathways we take to reach our final destinations.

However, there is a guiding light that always leads us to the right pathway; we have never been left in the darkness in our journey of life. Christ's unconditional love is that guiding light; it does not go out. In bad weather, it shines brighter. It does not matter what storm your marriage and family experience. Take courage. The storm cloud will disappear when you are connected to the power-generating plant of God's unconditional love, which illuminates the pathway to successful and joyful living.

I was born in a small, isolated district in Old Pera St. Thomas, Jamaica. The name of the district gives it a negative connotation but children from every family in this little area have acquired education, have traveled to foreign countries, and have experienced success. It does not matter where we are brought up. When we become adults, we are responsible for the pathways we choose. We have been given the potential power for greatness by our Creator. We can use our God-given ability to choose our destinations; the responsibility is ours. We need to learn how to make the right choices that will unleash our potential energy and harmonize our ability to succeed in our cultural and changing environment. We should never allow past experience to negatively influence our judgment.

When I was eleven years old, my parents moved from Old Pera to Lyssons, close to the town of Morant Bay, the capital of St. Thomas. I was the youngest of four children on my mother's side, and I also have six half-brothers and half-sisters from my father's side. My parents did their best to instill Christian virtue in my life and give me an education to start my journey.

As a teenager I was fascinated by some of the young men in my area. They were always surrounded by girls. I was brainwashed and impressed by their misguided exploitation of women. My dream was to get a job in Kingston, Jamaica, where I could meet all the lovely women. At age nineteen, I quit my job as a field assistant with the local municipality government in St. Thomas and moved to the big city of Kingston.

I got a job as a bus conductor, traveling from Kingston to Grange Hill, Westmoreland. For the first three months on the job, I thought I was enjoying myself. I met some intriguing and interesting women. I also was fascinated with older women, and it seemed as if they were drawn to me. I was overwhelmed yet elated by the new lifestyle. Deep within my mind, however, I knew that this lifestyle could not take me to the real pathway. I believed in moving up the ladder of success, and working as a conductor on a bus, collecting money from passengers, and chasing women was not the lifestyle for me—socially, morally, intellectually, or financially. I made the decision that this was not the path I wanted to travel. My religious background encouraged me to respect women; they represented my mother and sisters. My father taught me that women were to be treated with dignity and respect.

Many of my friends were fathering children with different women without taking responsibility for their actions. I made a decision that I would never father a child and allow him or her to grow up with a single parent. In this journey of life, God always spiritually directs our paths. He always says to follow the road that leads to eternal life. He does not dictate to us, but he always speaks in a still, soothing voice. If we pause a moment and listen, we will recognize his voice. His direction for us is the path that leads to success, but the choice is ours to make. Why not take the right path?

Just as water takes the shape of the pipe it flows through, life principles flow through us according to the nature of our thoughts. God's infinite wisdom always flows through our minds as harmony, health, peace, joy, and abundant love. Think and believe that it is continually flowing through you, and it will inspire and motivate your action. You will respond according to his mental and spiritual integrity. In life, the action and reaction of rest and motion must be balanced to provide equilibrium. In our journey of life, we should allow intellectual and positive emotion to flow through our minds to provide harmony and equilibrium—that will help balance our lives and lifestyles.

I am inviting all married couples, families, and friends to walk a mile with "T" and me, as we walk with the Lord in faith and belief in his creative power. If we can conceive the thing we want to accomplish, imagine it to be true, really think about it, and truly believe we can experience it, we will experience it. Our abilities to imagine, think, and believe are infinite in nature. That's true because God, our Father, is the creator of the universe, and he is in control of nature. He controls all things, visible and invisible. He is omnipresent, omnipotent, and the eminent one who provides equilibrium to our finite minds. He promises to supply all our needs, present and future. "But my God shall supply all your needs according to his riches in glory by Christ Jesus" Philippians 4:9 KJV).

It is good news if we believe it and not so good news if we don't believe it. It depends on what we conceive, imagine, think, believe, and perceive to be true in life. Our imaginations, our thoughts, and our beliefs are not only vast, but they're quite diverse. We all have our own individual ideas and opinions about what's right or wrong, good or bad, real or unreal, true or false. We have to consciously focus our minds and visualize the infinite power of God. "Finally, brethren, whatsoever things are true, whatsoever things are noble, whatsoever things are just, whatsoever things are pure, whatsoever things are lovely, whatsoever things are of good report; if there be any virtue, and if there be any praiseworthy—meditate on these things" (Philippians 4:8 NKJV).

The way we look at, judge, and perceive our experiences will determine the success of our marriages and families. Life will become successful if we truly believe and take action to make meaningful changes in our thinking and lifestyles. Our beliefs and perceptions about life are not necessarily true if our attitudes and behaviors contradict what we say or think. In life, everything has potential, including energy, but it can't help us unless it is put to work.

I have worked as a power engineer for fifteen years, so I know about the capability of potential energy. Wives and husbands have the potential ability to experience wonderful, loving, and caring married lives. The source of power is always available. It is for us to stay connected to God's infinite power source. As we leap into the twenty-first century, we will observe that the revolutionary concepts of marriage and family have been challenged. To begin our journey, I must let you know of the importance of professional marriage counselors who provide unique advice. Young couples who are planning to get married and married couples who are having marital problems should seek professional counseling. Our modern lifestyle has placed a heavy burden on marriage and family. This article on marriage and family posted on a Catholic website asked a relevant question:

> Does the consumer culture affect marriage? Yes it's devastating. Marriage is becoming a lifestyle with a person I choose because they can meet my needs and we can be happy together. I don't believe people bring this attitude to the altar. *(Catholic 2006, 16)*

Permit me to take you on an expedition in search of the real joyful marriage and family lifestyle. Come along with me on this unique treasure hunt. "Beloved I pray that you may prosper in all things and be in health, just as your soul prospers" (3 John 1:2 NKJV). On this journey of life, you will discover the good, the bad, and the ugly—divorce, abandoned family and children, depression, crime, and people drifting on the highway of life with no hope and no intended destination. Some are speeding recklessly without regard for their safety or the safety of their family and others. The following was written by an abandoned person:

> Family is who we look to when we need help. We expect our parents to raise us, our grandparents to love us, and our brothers and sisters to always be there for us when the chips are down. They are our blood, and we depend on that connection. When a family member doesn't live up to our expectations, we feel abandoned. When a parent, grandparent, or older brother or sister puts their needs in front of our own, we feel abandoned and alone. In such a case, we are likely to feel sad, alone, and angry.

However, on this treasure hunt, we are not searching for those things that destroy marriages, families, and lives—all those conditions that rob us of healthy and wealthy family relationships instead of bringing abundant blessings of infinite joy, peace, contentment, and serenity that strengthen our marriages and family treasures.

Many years ago, I was one of those people who was drifting on the highway of life, searching for happiness in all the wrong places. Sometimes I thought I had found it but alas, it eluded me all the way. My friends, happiness is a mood that comes and goes. It rises and it falls. Things and happenings do not provide real joyful living. We may accept grief, sadness, failure, and helplessness, but these things lead to sickness, disease, and destruction of joyful relationships. We need to move toward lifestyles that support our marriages and families and contribute love and compassion to our communities and society.

Overwhelming evidence suggests that the cause of many broken marriages is lifestyle-related. This should suggest that we should not focus all our time, energy, and effort on accumulating material things. We should be more concerned with lifestyle and the effect it could have on our physical, mental, spiritual, and emotional well-being. "Seek first the Kingdom and His righteousness, and all these things will be added unto you" (Matthew 6:33 NKJV). Many people have dedicated their lives to the search for things and happenings to find happiness, which allows them to lose focus of the real treasure.

Our conscious and subconscious minds crave joyful living, which provides contentment and lasting relationships that are built on the foundation of God's love and support of family and friends. We have become a generation of overstressed, intoxicated, and addicted people, speeding recklessly on the slippery highway of life, searching for something that we have never seen or experienced. It has driven many of us crazy, searching for something that is not tangible.

The result can be seen in our so-called marriages and families that are traveling dangerously on the wrong side of the highway of life and are spiraling out of control. Clouds of anxiety float in our mental skies. Mental hospitals are full of people who are suffering from depression and other stress-related diseases because of marital and family problems. The attitude on today's super-highway of life is scary. A reckless sense of urgency is demonstrated by most commuters. They want to get to their destinations of material success—now. There is no avenue for delayed gratification. The attitude is for getting it now, by any means, at any cost. It does not matter who gets hurt in the process. Many married couples say, "We cannot allow children to dictate our life." We should remember that children have no control or choice of coming into this world. They did not choose their parents; therefore, we should not let them become the victims of our indiscretion and unforgiving and rebellious spirits.

> Divorce introduces a massive change into the life of a boy or girl no matter what the age. Witnessing loss of love between parents, having parents break their marriage commitment, adjusting to going back and forth between two different households, and the daily absence of one parent while living with the other, all create a challenging new family circumstance in which to live. In the personal history of the boy or girl, parental divorce is a watershed event. Life that follows is significantly changed from how life was before. *(Pickhardt 2011)*

We need to develop a positive consciousness of the importance of a healthy marriage and a healthy family environment. Each of us is made up of trillions of cells, structured together to shape, design, and support of our minds and bodies. These cells cooperate and work harmoniously together to keep us alive. Our physical structures are composed of these building blocks from head to toe, including our hair, skin, blood, glands, and bones. Our entire bodies are made up of cells, and we are only as healthy as our cells. Like the cells, we are a community of people who are placed in this world as the foundation for growth and development of our families and our communities. When the cells in our minds and bodies communicate and function as units, we stay healthy and strong. If there is a communication breakdown, the cells become rogue cells, creating biological "crime," so to speak, which leads to disease and death.

The same phenomenal scenarios occur when married couples and families lose focus, and communication breaks down. Everything becomes disorganized, and there is potential for disaster—marital and family roadblocks on the highway of life.

When there is a road block, all commuters are affected. It does not matter which direction you are traveling; many accidents are caused by rubber-neckers (people who turn their heads to see what is happing on the other side of the highway). We should not allow our lifestyles to become negative distractions that could lead to danger for others.

Before you make decisions, remember that your choices will have a negative or positive effect on others. Consciously choose to make the right decisions. In life, we do not have any control over tomorrow. Enjoy today, and do not worry about tomorrow—it may not come. Live in the present, not in the past. Yes, you need to make plans for the future, but do not waste your energy on worrying. A large percentage of the things most of us worry about never happen. Families need to take more time to worship together, play together, laugh together, and find joy in loving relationships. Wives and husbands need to demonstrate the same love and affection they shared when they first met.

Relive those joyful moments as often as you can. They will rekindle the passion and energize and revitalize affection and tender loving care. Your brain has neurotransmitters that need those joyful messages. They feed and nurture your emotional neural pathways and your limbic system to refresh your memory of the wonderful things you've shared with others. Be mindful of the thoughts you entertain. Exercising positive thinking indicates that you're paying attention to the minute things that assist you in keeping your internal focus, as opposed to permitting your mind to wander. When you're overly cautious and worry about what happened yesterday or the day before, you reside in the past and allow distracting thoughts to pass through your mind, which then does not allow precious moments of joyful living to sustain your marriage and family.

Being mindful is important, as it can help to reduce stressful moments, induce positive thinking, and influence how you use your own energy to manage and obtain what you desire in your marriage and family, including a richer, happier, joyful mental state. Simple strategies, such as being mindful of others, could help you to become more conscious of God's promised blessings. Be an optimist as you journey life's pathway. Take advantage of every opportunity to nurture your marriage and family and truly believe that together, you will conquer difficulties and defeat failure. Winston Churchill famously said, "A pessimist sees the difficulty in every opportunity; an optimist sees the opportunity in every difficulty."

Joyful married life—whether you equate it with happiness, optimism, well-being, personal achievement, or all of the above—goes hand in hand with healthier habits, attitudes, and behaviors. My personal experience shows that when a wife and husband enjoy their marriage relationship and are in good spirits, they tend to pray together, eat better, exercise more frequently, and get better sleep and are more emotionally balanced than those who do not enjoy their marriages. This could be, in part, because leading a healthy married lifestyle helps to achieve the goal of real joyful living, which can eliminate incidence of separation and divorce that is so common in the modern environment. It could also be that a successful marriage leads to better health, which in turn lends itself to a better mood and joyful living.

Beyond these rather common-sense associations, however, is an intriguing reality that supports the fact that when you are united in real love and affection, a joyful and happy relationship makes you healthy and wealthy—spiritually, mentally, physically, and financially—and allows you to be emotionally balanced. It also tends to lead to better eating, exercise, and other healthy habits, and it supports the suggestion that a positive mental state may has a direct effect on your mind and body. A successful marriage creates joyful habits that influence your neurotransmitters, your immune function, and much more, and it stimulates positive thinking. The result is a joyful and loving marriage and family relationship that encourage you to stay together, regardless of any difficult times.

> A major survey of 127,545 American adults found that married men are healthier than men who were never married or whose marriages ended in divorce or widowhood. Men who have marital partners also live longer than men without spouses; men who marry after age 25 get more protection than those who tie the knot at a younger age and the longer a man stays married, the grater his survival advantage over his unmarried peers. *(Harvard Men's Health Watch 2010)*

My elder sister, Phyllis Johnson, has been married for over fifty-one years. Her husband, William, is experiencing memory loss. He only feels comfortable and relaxes when he is with her, because she knows how to take care of him. My niece Sylvia Mackenzie has been married for more than forty years. Her husband, Lloyd, had a massive stroke. Most people believed he would be confined to bed or a wheelchair for the rest of his life, but Sylvia's support and tender loving care motivated and inspired him to walk again. Loving and caring spouses who support their partners in good times and in bad times fulfill their vows—"for better or for worse, until death do we part."

One study found that happiness, optimism, life satisfaction, and other positive psychological attributes are associated with a lower risk of heart disease. Marriage and family are designed to provide joyful, intimate relationships, which equate to abundant blessing. "Love suffers long, and is kind; love does not envy; love does not parade itself, is not puffed up, does not behave rudely, does not seek its own, is not provoked, thinks no evil; does not rejoice in iniquity, but rejoices in the truth; bears all things, believes all things, hope all things, endures all things. Love never fails" (1 Corinthians 13:4–8 NKJV).

As I sat down to write, I asked myself how I could make a difference in these difficult times. So many lives are affected by the economic and social tidal waves and lifestyle disasters that wash over marital and family values. The answer came to me: my lifestyle can make a difference. So I decided to share our fifty-year marriage experience with as many people as I can reach through the written word and generate an essence of sweet aroma to marriages, families, and friends. By doing so, I also will strengthen my faith and belief in my Creator's unconditional love, which transmits abundant, joyful living.

We all need to practice the Golden Rule: do unto others as you would have them do unto you. From all the reports I have seen, recklessness, selfishness, and greed are the cause of the economic train wreck that affects marriages and families.

Let us pledge allegiance to God, our country, and community by making mental, physical, spiritual, and emotional lifestyle changes that will rekindle our patriotic compassion and love, demonstrated by Christ and many of our forefathers. The touch of his love will allow our marriages to transcend the boundaries of mediocrity, lifestyle conflicts, social norms, conventional wisdom, and financial burdens and will elevate our minds and hearts on the glorious promise that Christ will be with us in all our challenges. "Fear not, for I am with you; be not dismayed, for I am your God. I will strengthen you, yes I will help you, I will uphold you with My righteous right hand" (Isaiah 41:10 NKJV). His promises never fail. Just a touch of his garment will provide healing to our struggles. He has the answer to all our questions and desires.

A woman who was suffering from bleeding for twelve years found a true miracle. Her faith remained healthy. She believed that she could be well again, despite all evidence to the contrary. When she heard about a man who'd "healed many who had various diseases" (Mark 1:34), she made every effort to reach out and touch his garment. Those of us who believe in God's promises should remember that he says, "Whatsoever ye shall ask in prayer, believing, ye shall receive" (Matthew 21:22). Those who are not believers should try this recipe of faith in Christ's promises.

Marriage counselors and psychologists are overworked, trying to fix our problems. My own endless drifting came to a halt when I was confronted with the reality the prodigal son's experience. I realized that if I did not change direction, I would self-destruct. I was invited to an educational seminar on men's health, where I saw a number of graphic images of young men and women whose lives were devastated by venereal diseases (sexually transmitted diseases) The images helped me to realize that people's lifestyles can expose them to these life-changing diseases and the dangerous effects. I took a detour home, where I sought comfort in prayer and the direction I should take in life.

You see, I was from a religious home, where my parents were believers of a Christian faith. I used to go to the Baptist church with my mother and the Catholic church with my cousin, whom I visited on some weekends. In these churches I learned moral virtue and spiritual values. In my prayers, I reached out in faith and desperately touched Christ's garment, hoping that his virtue would transcend my weakness and provide strength to satisfy my needs. In my prayer, I asked God for three specific things:

1) A good job
2) A caring and loving wife
3) To be led to the right church

I ended my prayer by thanking God for answering my prayer. This prayer was sincere, because I realized I needed a new direction in life, and I could not find it without divine help. Many times in the journey of life, we need to reach out in faith and claim his promises. Doubt, in many instances, prevents us from touching his garment in faith, moment by moment. My simple prayer was answered in the same order I requested. I got a job at the Government of Jamaica Post Office.

About three months later, on a beautiful Sunday morning, as I was about to board a city bus, I looked over my shoulder—and there she was. I had my Jacob experience. The moment Jacob saw Rachel, he knew that he had found the woman he would love for the rest of his life. At that moment, I experienced Jacob's willingness to work for seven years for his bride. I made a decision, then and there, that I must find a way to make the acquaintance of this lovely, beautiful, and charming young lady. I started planning the best strategy for getting her attention.

I stepped back to allow her to get on the bus. After desperately maneuvering and using tactful ingenuity, I got a seat beside her. From my personal experience, I knew that a young lady would not normally appreciate a man trying to make her acquaintance on public transportation, so I waited for an opportune moment. I was prepared to risk introducing myself because I felt it was well worth it. Before I could say anything, however, Providence took over. I believe God intervened to bring us together, because something spectacular happened at that very moment that caused everyone on the bus to start talking to each other—an insane man streaked down the street. In the moment of excitement, I seized the opportunity to start a conversation, which allowed me to introduce myself to her.

She was hesitant but polite. It was a long journey, and I proved myself to be a gentleman by using all the right words, which was acceptable to this beautiful young lady. At the end of the journey, she gave me her address, because like Jacob and Rachel, we were drawn together by divine inspiration and guidance. That evening, I rushed over to my favorite cousin's house. I told her I would like her to meet a lovely young lady with whom I was hoping to get better acquainted. She informed me that her church was starting a series of meetings, and she would be delighted if I could attend and invite my new acquaintance.

Immediately after leaving my cousin Joy, I visited the special young lady and invited her to the meeting. She willingly accepted my invitation. To my greatest delight, after introducing her to my cousin Joy, both were drawn to each other. They acted as if they were long-lost friends. We went to the meeting. At the end of the presentation, the pastor made an appeal to the congregation, requesting those of us who were not baptized to give our hearts to God. I responded to the appeal. To my delight, Theresa, my date to the meeting, did the same. We continued to attend the series of meetings.

The church members were kind and loving to us. Three months after attending the first meeting, we got baptized and became members of the congregation of our newfound faith. The church members became our family and friends. Their love and caring Christian friendship helped to sustain our faith in God and his church and guided us to the right highway on life's journey. As we have journeyed together, we've enjoyed God's bountiful blessings and an intimate relationship that has allowed us to experience the power of God's grace and his tender loving care, which envelops our life.

The Lord added to our blessing four wonderful, beautiful children—two girls and two boys. I was twenty-three, and Theresa was twenty-one years old when we got married. The Rollington Town Seventh-day Adventist Church members and my cousin Joy (Hutton) Harris will always have a special place in our hearts.

In your life's journey, your kindness, love, and caring spirit are qualities that provide blessing, strength, and comfort to many weary travelers who seek rest and direction to the Promised Land, where we all will never grow weary or old. Whenever difficult challenges enter your path, remember that you are not alone; Christ is just a prayer away. Dial him up, and he will take your call. You will never be too early or too late. The time of the day or night does not matter. He is never too busy to take your call.

When Theresa and I got engaged, all our church family wanted to take an active part in our wedding. Some gave fatherly or motherly advice. Others shared in the planning. We were elated with the attention given to us and were relieved of the stress that many young couples experience when planning their weddings. The night before the wedding, I could not sleep. I lay in bed, counting every second and minute. I had asked Theresa to promise me that she would be at the church on time for our wedding. I was eager to get the celebration over. I had been waiting patiently for my wife for one year. People told me it would be the "bride's day"; I just would be the guy standing at the altar, waiting to say "I do." Our wedding was a small one, but many family members and friends put in time and energy to share the wonderful moment with us. Christ and the heavenly host celebrated with us when we took that special vow and asked for his blessing.

After our wedding, I continued to work at the general post office, and Theresa went to nursing school. After her graduation, she got a job at the George Fifth Memorial Sanatorium in Kingston. After I'd worked for six years at the general post office, I got a new job with the Ministry of Housing as a housing officer.

I was assigned to a branch office in Lyssons, St. Thomas (my hometown), and Theresa took a job at Princess Margaret

Hospital in Lyssons. This was God's guidance and added blessing, because I was back home. We also had the privilege of living in the late prime minister's (Sir Alexander Bustamante's) beach cottage. The rent was ridiculously low, because my father was managing the property. My family enjoyed a lovely home, located on over ten acres of land by the beach. We had the privilege of having our relatives, church family, and friends visit with us, spending time on the beach.

At night, we could listen to the rhythmic crashing of the waves and see the moonlight reflecting on the ocean. In the morning, we listened to the chirruping of the birds and whistling music of the wind as it traveled through the leaves of the trees, adding to the soothing sounds of nature, which ignited a romantic atmosphere that brought comfort and joy to our marriage and young family.

My wife and I enjoyed the new and refreshing blessing of worshipping with the members of the Morant Bay Seventh-day Adventist Church in the country environment, closer to nature and solitude, which relieved us from the concrete jungle and congested traffic of the large city. In our humble walk together, with Christ as our guide, we learned and gained knowledge and strength from simple and sometime dramatic incidents. We were young students in marriage, and we did not want to display an attitude of wise fools. We sought divine guidance. We knew that we should always seek blessing and counsel from God's words. "And we know that all things work together for good to those who love God, to those who are called according to his purpose" (Romans 8:28 NKJV).

I can vividly remember a special incident that occurred one evening. After giving my wife a driving lesson, she drove us to the nurses' residence to visit her friends. Some of the nurses were sitting on the lawn near the building. Theresa was a little excited to see her friends. She meant to stop the car, but she applied the gas pedal instead of the brake, and the car ran into the wall of the building. I was upset because our new car was damaged, and I was worried about the cost to repair it.

I took a deep breath and quickly got out of the car. I rushed to the driver's side, opened the door, and helped Theresa out of the car. She was shaking with fright and embarrassment and was fearful of the extent of the damage to the car. I restrained my anger, hugged her, and said, "Don't worry, my love. You are more important than the car. Thank God you are not hurt. The car is metal, and it can be repaired." The nurses started cheering and said, "That is so sweet."

A great smile broke out on Theresa's face. My anger turned to joy, and the words I spoke became precious jewels to me and my wife. From that day, I was a respected husband and gentleman to all the nurses. They mentioned the incident to their friends who were not present. When you show respect for your wife or husband, you mold and strengthen your marriage and your character, and you nurture your mental and emotional health and well-being. I gained respect from my wife and her friends, and many of the nurses were impressed by our actions.

What if I had stepped out of that car and reacted angrily and said the wrong words? My wife would have been devastated. I would have damaged my self-respect and my Christian values. My wife would have been upset with herself and me. She would have questioned her driving skill. Her confidence was boosted by my action. She got her driver's license the first time she went for her test. How we react to incidents can have negative or positive effects on our spouses, families, and the people with whom we associate.

Theresa told me that she is a better driver than I am, because she got her license the first time she took the test, but it took me three tries to get my license. I told her she did well on the test because I was an excellent teacher. We enjoy such relaxing moments of teasing and having fun with each other. Many marriages have failed because people say the wrong things before thinking of the consequences.

The following children's story is very meaningful for me. It was told by Pastor Frank at the New Life SDA Church in Oshawa, Ontario:

There once was a little boy who had a bad temper. When he didn't get what he wanted, he would start to shout and cry; sometimes he would even fall on the ground, yelling. Other times, he would have a bad attitude and would not do as his parents asked. Well, one day, the little boy's father gave him a bag of nails and told him that every time he lost his temper, he must hammer a nail into the back of the fence. He would lose his temper, and out he would go to put in a nail in the fence. He got angry again and told Mommy no when she told him to do something. Another nail was hammered. The nails weren't easy to drive in, so he tried to behave better, but an hour later, he didn't get his way and began to scream and cry. Out he went again to hammer a nail! At the end of the first day, the boy had driven thirty-seven nails into the fence! But over the next few weeks, as he learned to control his anger, the number of nails he had to hammer in daily went down. He discovered it was easier to hold his temper than to drive those nails into the fence. Finally, the day came when the boy didn't lose his temper at all. He told his father about it, and the father suggested that the boy now pull out one nail for each day that he was able to hold his temper. So every day he didn't get mad, he would pull a nail out of the fence. The days passed, and finally one day, the young boy was able to tell his father that all the nails were gone. The father took his son by the hand and led him to the fence. The wise father had one more lesson to teach his son. He said, "You've done well, my son, but look at the fence where you pulled out the nails. What do you see?" The boy saw holes from the nails. The father said, "The fence will never be the same. When you say things in anger, they leave a scar just like this one. No matter how many times you say sorry for hurting someone, the wound you caused is still there. Hurting someone with your words can hurt just as bad as hurting them with your fists. So learn to control your anger."

And so the little boy learned a big lesson that day. How many times have you hurt someone with unkind words? The attitude you have—whether you are kind and gentle or hurtful and angry—leaves its mark on people. Jesus himself had holes in his body from the nails hammered in. As Jesus said, learn to treat others as you want others to treat you. Learn to treat people with kindness. When you fail to extend to others the love you require for yourself, you defeat your ability to demonstrate God's unconditional love in your mind and heart. Reflect Christ's character in your lifestyle.

The choices you make influence your search for a joyful and successful marriage and family life. It is rewarding to follow the path of love, respect, and compassion for each other. Love is contagious, so why not use your love to flood your friends and community? It will be an excellent fragrance for your environment.

> The link between a bad marriage and heart disease is more pronounced for older couples and, in particular, women, finds a study led by Michigan State University. Older couples in a bad marriage - particularly female spouses - have a higher risk for heart disease than those in a good marriage, finds the first nationally representative study of its kind. *(Science Daily 2014)*

On the rugged terrain of life's journey, there are many difficult challenges, and you must navigate your way through a maze of obstacles—both negative and positive factors. Theresa and I made a decision before we got married that no matter what differences we had, we would not go to bed before speaking to each other and coming to some neutral understanding. We've made some mistakes—there is never a perfect marriage or a perfect wife or husband—but we never allowed our challenges to develop into problems that could destroy our marriage. Sometimes the pathways are difficult to travel, but those are the ones that leave a lasting impression and help to mold, shape, and strengthen our relationship. Wives and husbands need to learn conflict resolution. I have learned from comments that people make, positive or negative.

In church or any function I attend, I always sit with my family. If I have to leave because I have another commitment, I excuse myself and return as soon as possible. Many wives say that their husbands do not sit with their families during church services and social gatherings. We need to set an example for our children and our young people, who are looking to us for guidance. Mothers and fathers have a responsibility to teach their sons and daughters how to love and respect their spouses. Our actions are more powerful than body language or verbal language.

In our world, communication and messages come to us through sensory channels that guide our paths. We were created with the unique ability to understand and interpret the nature of our environments and to enjoy rich natural resources and fundamental blessings. We have been taught the meaning of these sensory experiences and how society expects us to respond to them. Our interpretation and understanding of language gives us the ability to be sensitive to our spouses, our families, and the people around us. Body language and verbal language, however, are often very specific. When we learn to combine the experiences of our five senses with verbal language, we create a dynamic communication system. Early in life, we learn to create visual and verbal messages, but little—if any—time is spent in learning what is going on around us and how to use them to increase our understanding and communication about the world around us. That will allow us to be more sensitive to our loved ones and their special needs. We need to examine our inner senses, such as feelings, emotions, sensations, and perception of our social environments.

Technology allows us to create more elaborate user-friendly communication gadgets that prevent us from using our sensory God-given language skills. Lack of using our senses may result in unintended or contradictory messages between the sensory channels of our bodies and the traditional channels of visual and verbal communication. This contradiction must not occur if we want to be more compassionate in dealing with another's needs. Human senses are an important way of communicating kindness and introducing and integrating the concept into a marriage and family lifestyle. Body language and our actions can convey more forceful messages than verbal language. Take time to examine the many ways you communicate with your spouse, children, and others. Many of the messages may be your attitude and reaction to your everyday challenges. If interpreted incorrectly, the messages could cause irreparable damage to others.

When I was planning to emigrate to Canada, many people suggested that I should go alone and send for my family after I had made preparations for them. I insisted that I would not leave my family. We would go together or stay in Jamaica, It is important that your nuclear family stick together. It does not matter what financial or other incentives attract your attention. Many families have made the mistake of separating temporarily to emigrate, and they never reunite as a family. Their intentions were good, but the challenges encountered became hazardous to marriage and family.

We are to guard against temptation. When we allow material things to take precedence over our intimate relationships of marriage and family, we set up ourselves for failure. My family emigrated to Canada together. We experienced some challenges, but they brought us closer together.

Theresa and I know that we are living in an environment that requires unity and teamwork, so that we can successfully build our relationship and sustain our love for each other. Couples who are willing to adjust to this unique environment must be willing to work together as a family and be sympathetic with each other's needs.

Our minds and bodies are a community of over one hundred trillion cells, which are the building blocks of our lives. These cells form tissues, organs, and systems. Each cell is like an individual; it can survive on its own. Cells, however, do not compete as we do; they cooperate. When cells are working and communicating efficiently, the human body experiences optimum health and wellness. If cells become defective, they lose the ability to communicate effectively. They will send the wrong messages, which could endanger the efficient operation of the human body. This could lead to sickness or death.

Marriage and family are like the cells. For our marriages and families to survive in this turbulent environment, we must learn to cooperate and communicate effectively. When there is a communication breakdown in our marriages and families, our relationships become sick and die. This adds more problems to our struggling family values and could become a burden to government and society. I believe that my Christian faith and the teaching of love and mercy reinforce and strengthen my desire and determination to be loving—and lovable—to my wife.

I feel that when Christian families separate, they send the wrong message to the world. In many instances, they are saying that they do not believe in what they preach. What messages do we send to our children and young people when they see their mothers or fathers walking into the church building, arm in arm with another man or woman, or they take home another man or woman to introduce to their children as their new mom or dad? I am not judging an individual's integrity. There are different reasons why wives and husbands separate, and some may be for just cause. Judgment of their actions is between them and God. For Theresa and me, however, I can say in humility that it feels so good to have reached our fiftieth anniversary! I feel empowered, energized, and elated that we have been given the opportunity, by God's grace, to continue our journey of life together.

When a wife and husband separate, in many instances, it is a mental and emotional decision. It is not spontaneous; many separations started the day after the honeymoon. The reality of the responsibility of being a wife, a husband, a father, or a mother can become a shock to some people. They were not ready to give up the freedom of doing what they wanted to do and going where they wanted to go. When we are married, our commitments change. We have to be committed to our marriages and families. When we start having children, we have to make adjustments. Young married couples have challenging decisions to make, and these can cause uncomfortable moments. Theresa and I learned by trial and error that these are learning experiences. Many of the wonderful inventions we enjoy today were achieved from trial and error. The inventors never gave up—if they had, we would not enjoy many of the technological blessings that have added to today's lifestyle.

Everything you do affect your children. From your views on sugary snacks to your way of slamming doors when your temper flares, everything you do teaches your children something. For the most part, you know that being a positive role model for your kids is imperative, but even if you don't drink, smoke, do drugs or engage in any form of physical abuse, your lifestyle might still negatively affect your kids. On the same note, your healthy lifestyle choices have just as much on your kids. *(Global Post 2015)*

When we marry, we have to leave those friends we use to hang out with. Our mothers, fathers, siblings, and other relatives should no longer influence our decisions and commitments. If you want to be with Mom and Dad, do not get married. Many marriages fail because of parental involvement. The good intentions of Mom and Dad can become destructive to their children's marriages and families. I must hasten to say that I am not referring to an abusive relationship. When there is abuse, parents and community have the right to intervene; it is our spiritual and moral obligation and responsibility.

In general, however, when a couple gets married and starts a family, involvement of the parents may be viewed as an unwanted intrusion. Parents should be the support base for their children. If the children ask for advice, parents should be willing to give it without prejudice.

Young couples, you should always entertain love and respect for your parents and in-laws. They have made lots of sacrifices to give you the opportunities to experience your new lives. Demonstrate compassion and love for your in-laws.

We should allow Christ's nurturing love in our marriages and families, to build and strengthen the immune system of our relationships. It will fight and defend against pathogens—those people who destroy marriages. Just as one hundred trillion communities of cells in the human body can cooperate and work harmoniously to provide optimum health and wellness, families, married couples, and others can communicate, cooperate, and work harmoniously together to provide a healthy and wealthy, loving and lovable, caring, joyful family relationship.

I have felt friendship and respect from most of my church family and friends, who are supportive when we experience difficult times. The challenge is for us to motivate, educate, and encourage this supportive lifestyle in our towns, cities, and communities. If we do this, we can make a difference in society and in our communities, and we will set an example for the world to mirror.

In a hectic and stressful environment, work and financial difficulties may challenge a family's values, but this should not stop the continuation of a family expedition in search of real joy in the relationship. My wife's and my Christian beliefs allow us to see the need for Christian families to cooperate with their communities to design plans that will assist young couples and other families who are experiencing difficulties, to eliminate or contain marital hazards before they contribute to incidents. A wife, husband, and family who have successfully traveled a marital pathway should be good tour guides. They could use their knowledge to assist others who are starting or planning for a successful expedition.

Governments established laws and procedures to protect wives, husbands, and families from abusive situations. These are commendable, but they are not the foundations that will sustain and strengthen our marriages and family relationships. We are the true builders and sustainers of our families and home environments. Our actions will determine the destiny of our families and marriages. We can be members of the construction crew that builds a strong foundation of a loving, caring family, or we can be the wrecking gang that destroys family values.

My Christian belief and experience allows me to stay on the highway that has taken Theresa and me to "Fiftieth Anniversary Boulevard," to celebrate with a unique group of families in a resort situated on Memory Lane. In the family resort, I have met couples who have traveled the highway for over sixty-one years. This is a statement of real success in action, demonstrated by men and women who have worked together in the rugged terrain of life's journey and have set an example for people to follow.

Many people know such wonderful families but do not recognize or learn from the bountiful blessings they display. To me, marriage and family provide the mental, physical, spiritual, and emotional balance that is the foundation of our Christian values, which enrich our society and the world.

Successful marriages and families provide harmony and love in our homes and communities and prevent prejudice, poverty, war, discontent, and broken dreams. They sustain joy, contentment, peace, and the serenity of an individual's inner self. We cannot allow bad attitudes and selfishness to cause anxiety that will defeat our performance. Wives, husbands, mothers, and fathers are builders, not wrecking gangs. Families should be mentally, physically, and emotionally prepared for emergencies, twenty-four/seven. You cannot allow your mind to be occupied with tension, anger, and resentment. These components are counterproductive and will create feelings such as fear, apprehension, or worry.

In the anatomy and physiology of family and marriage, symptoms of bad attitude, selfishness, and animosity could cause anxiety and are often accompanied by physical sensations, such as heart palpitations, nausea, chest pains, shortness of breath, stomachaches, or headaches. From a biological perspective, our minds and bodies are equipped to eliminate or contain the dangers they perceive, and they prepare organs of defense to deal with the threat, known as an "emergency reaction." Blood pressure and heart rate are increased, sweating is increased, blood flow to the major muscle groups is increased, and immune and digestive system functions are compromised. External signs of anxiety may include pale skin, sweating, trembling, and papillary dilation. Emotionally, anxiety causes a sense of dread or panic, and physically, it causes nausea and chills. Voluntary and involuntary behaviors may arise, with the intention of escaping or avoiding the source of anxiety—this often is the most extreme spontaneous reaction. However, anxiety is not always pathological or unstable. It is also a common emotion, along with fear, anger, sadness, and happiness, and it has a very important function in relation to our survival.

We are all blessed with the mental capacity to think and make decisions. It is our responsibility to accumulate resources that will aid and guide us from symptoms of bad attitude and other negative behaviors as we continue our search for joyful and successful marriages and family lifestyles.

Did you know that the brain contains over ten billion neurons, or brain cells, and between these brain cells are neurotransmitters? Neurotransmitters are chemical messengers that transmit thoughts, moods, and emotions from cell to cell, allowing our brain cells to communicate efficiently with each other. These neurotransmitters also send messages to the nervous, endocrine, immune, and other systems to promote growth and harmony. One of the blessings of being human is that we experience emotions. How we feel is directed by certain neurotransmitters. These neurotransmitters change regularly between our brain cells to meet the needs of our present circumstances.

Think of this important factor: at night, to induce sleep, it necessary for our brains to rise to a certain level of awareness. Our thoughts are transmitted in a calming, quieting, and relaxing manner so that we can sleep well. Always affirm that you are in perfect peace and harmony with your loved ones and others. To live harmoniously with others is beneficial for you and your health and for the health of your marriage and family. Many people believe that love revolves around the heart. The heart is a symbol of love, but in essence, it is the brain that generates chemical signals to make you understand the emotion of love that is needed for holistic balance of mind and body.

In the morning, your brain must lower the level of these neurotransmitters and raise other excitatory transmitters' levels. If, for some reason, you did not sleep well because you were in conflict with your spouse or under mental stress, these very important brain functions are put out of balance, and you wake up as a totally dysfunctional person, with an attitude that could lead to a negative incident that might affect your life and the lives of your family and coworkers. When you sleep well—because you are at peace with others and enjoying life, marriage, family, and friends—your brain's neurotransmitters increase levels of euphoria. This positive attitude will eliminate the desire for illegal substances and other negative factors that affect family relationships. During times of stress, your brain must raise levels of the transmitters that help you to be alert and in control. The brain is resilient, but it needs your cooperation to function efficiently. Never say, "I am stressed," or "I'm depressed." When you do, you are saying that this is what you *are*. You are not depressed or stressed, but you may *feel* stressed or depressed. You are a mind, body, and spirit that has the potential ability to take control of your life.

Remember, love occurs in the brain, which generates chemical signals to make you understand the spiritual discernment of God's unconditional love. Your mind, brain, and body work seamlessly together to keep your behavior in a balance. "For God hath not given us a spirit of fear; but of power, and of love, and of a sound mind" (2 Timothy 1:7 NKJV).

If your brain is contaminated with hazardous material, such as discontent, animosity, fear, fatigue, stress, or drugs, you become defenseless in responding when there is an emergency. It is critical that all of the major neurotransmitters be present in your brain daily and in sufficient amounts, so that your brain will be chemically, physically, spiritually, and emotionally in balance. When there are insufficient amounts of one or more neurotransmitters, the ratio is upset, and negative symptoms are experienced.

Leslie Hart, author of *Human Brain and Human Learning*, has identified six major patterns of the brain. These are tools that can be used as a support base for marriage and family.

They are:

- Objects—how do you perceive the objects around you? Can they be used as tools to build your marriage and family relationship?
- Actions—the actions you take to develop a loving and caring marriage and family relationship.
- Procedures—the procedures you use to resolve conflict and develop strategies to strength your marriage relationship.
- Situations—you encounter these every moment of your life. How can you analyze, evaluate, and use them to build your marriage relationship?
- Relationships—the relationships you share with your spouse and family are key to successful joyful living.
- System—developed within your marriage and family environment are mental, spiritual, physical, and emotional support for joyful living.

We can use our brains and learning abilities to develop strategies to communicate and cooperate in supporting each other; to provide strength, stability, and a strong foundation; to emotionally eliminate defeat; to establish a productive and balanced family order, where love and harmony rule; and to develop an atmosphere of unique discipline that will lead to a real, meaningful, healthy and wealthy lifestyle.

The human body has twenty-nine core muscles that are the foundation for movement. Strengthening them can help protect and support your back, make your spine and body less prone to injury, and help you gain greater balance and stability. In your marriage and family, you can use eighteen core words to provide strength and stability to secure the foundation of your marriage and family. These words are love, joy, peace, hope, patience, kindness, goodness, faithfulness, compassion, mercy, forgiveness, trust, belief, faith, integrity, and assertiveness. You can add others to your vocabulary. Words are like bricks that are used for the building of marriage and family. Action is the cement that holds the bricks together, and attitude is the paint that enhances its beauty. These core words could provide a solid foundation of support and security and could build a lifestyle for marriage and family that displays the tranquility of joyful living. Use these words as affirmation to maintain healthy, wealthy, joyful living. Bible texts can complement these words; use them for daily affirmation. They will give you a marital balance and foundation that will stand the test of time.

2

Lifestyle Factors

I have learned that a change in lifestyle begins with me—with my perception and how I view things around me. How can I influence my surroundings? Change is not about the other person. It is about me. It is about you. Always remember that you can make a difference. Relish the diversity and challenges of the people around you. Benefit from the opportunity to connect with like-minded people. Do not be afraid of resistance, of people who oppose you, or of your competitors. They are not your enemies. They provide you with an opportunity to redouble your efforts and endurance so that you can become better at what you do. In life, there is good attitude and bad attitude. Tap into the resources of the infinite wisdom and knowledge of God's words daily. Develop an attitude of flexibility and resilience to achieve positive outcomes, and eliminate a negative attitude before it becomes a systemic, discriminatory behavior that could destroy your marriage and family.

A structured family learns to respect the individual needs of each family member. Practice open communication, which is highly valued. This unselfish structure is flexible rather than rigid. Open communication is desirable and allows family members to be more relaxed and to feel appreciated. In such a structured environment, husband and wife offer explanations, not condemnations. They encourage confidence and love, not fear. They encourage self-confidence in the family environment, which energizes and motivates individual self-esteem. They uphold the family values and eliminate deviant behavior. When rational values are standard and encouraged, emotional and spiritual values are nurtured.

There is also a need to go back to the Christian beliefs of the early settlers in the United States and Canada and many of our Western cultures. The foundation of their belief was interconnected with God and family values. This is demonstrated every year by Thanksgiving celebrations, where families come together to give thanks for their bountiful blessings. "So God created man in his own image; in the image of God created him; male and female he created them" (Genesis 1:27). "And the Lord God said, 'It is not good that man should be alone; I will make him a help comparable to him'" (Genesis 2:18 NKJV).

Marriage is the structure of the family relationship, which is built on the foundation of God's unconditional love. In our world today, this principle is deteriorating. As the family structure goes, so goes the morality of our society—this is evidenced by escalating crime, violence, and health problems, which are stressful to our marriages, families, and society.

We are images of God's character, and the Bible says God is love. Therefore, I conclude that we all have the potential power to love. Christ also says, "You shall love the lord thy God with all your heart, with all your soul, and with your entire mind. This is the first and great commandment. And the second is like it, you shall love thy neighbors as thyself" (Matthew 22:37–39 NKJV). In our world today, the emphasis is on making love. Physical encounters may last for a few minutes, and then the excitement is over. David's son's love of passion for his sister ended up in disaster, because it was lust, not love. Lustful behavior leads to a destructive end. There are no plans for the aftereffects. Many sexually transmitted diseases are the result of these casual physical encounters. Children become victims of our indiscretions. This was not God's plan for his people.

Most of these indiscretions become a burden to the health care system and the country. Sex is a precious, beautiful, and unique gift from God, to solidify a marriage relationship between a man and a woman. Sex has many healing virtues. It can heal, and it also can kill. We should not destroy its sacredness. Sex can become a weapon of mass destruction, destroying marriages and families when used for selfish pleasure.

I want to thank God for my wife—my love, my friend, and my companion for fifty years, who has provided me with tender loving care. We walk together hand in hand, with Christ guiding us on the pathway of life's journey. We would like to be the reflection of his guiding light, illuminating the way to a healthy and wealthy lifestyle. Families must nurture and build a healthy and wealthy society. Therefore, incentives are needed to encourage and promote healthy lifestyle changes—lifestyles that will unite marriages and families, govern our lives, enrich the integrity of our families, and strengthen our characters from inside out, to display the beauty and quality of a Christ-like character.

We must rebuild our relationships with God, our families, our neighbors, and our communities. If you do not have a relationship with God or do not learn to love your wife, who is grafted to you, becoming one in flesh, how can you love your neighbors? Your body is the temple of God. If you destroy your temple, you destroy your relationship with the Creator. Many of us destroy our minds and bodies with unhealthy lifestyles. Let us continue our search for joyful living.

Joyful living is the confident assurance of God's love in our lives. Happiness is the outward expression of joyful living. Happiness depends on things and circumstances, but joyful living depends on Jesus. If things and happenings provide happiness, what happens when circumstances change, loved ones die, marriages fail, money is lost, health deteriorates, and the party is over? Happiness takes a vacation, and depression takes over. But for those of us who have a relationship with our families and God, there is contentment, serenity, and peace from knowing and experiencing Jesus's love, personally.

We are placed in this world to be good stewards of all the world's resources. We are designed with gifts and talents to be used to the best of our ability, for sustaining our families, ourselves, and our communities and our country. As John F. Kennedy said in his 1961 Inaugural Address, "Ask not what your country can do for you—ask what you can do for your country." The ability to use all these gifts and talents comes with special responsibilities and training. We should be temperate and efficient in managing our resources, including our time and our talents. We were created to rule over the animals, not to behave like them. We were given the ability to think and to reason and arrive at an intelligent decision. Animals were given instincts for survival. When we accept the concept of survival of the fittest, we indicate that we are changing the characteristics and uniqueness of our Creator's image that has been given to us. We should be careful not to become too emotionally sensitive and create a mental perception that could disrupt the potential flow of energy. Unleash your infinite wisdom and allow the love of God to guide and sustain your marriage and family relationship.

Many people complain of being tired, fearful, depressed, or stressed out because of their lifestyle. The amount of stress that our minds and bodies can tolerate before the chemical balance of the mind malfunctions is referred to as "stress tolerance." Negative or sad messages are factors that could cause imbalance. Feed your mind with joyful, nurturing messages of hope and faith in the spirit of love. Sad messages weaken your ability to think positively, and they defeat optimism. We may become pessimistic, always seeing the glass as half empty rather than half full. When we play the "blame game," we say a situation or event was the other person's fault. We fail to take responsibility. It is imperative that we grow rich in faith, belief, and hope in the spirit of love and that we use these things, given to us by God, to provide financial stability for our families. Do not allow anyone to cheat you out of these blessings and satisfaction. They are gifts from God.

There is an abundant blessing in providing service to our families and to people in our community and our country. To accumulate knowledge and material things to use for our family and in service to others is a blessing that should be used to provide stability—mental, spiritual, physical, and financial. We need to follow the Golden Rule, but do not let anyone make you feel guilty for your marriage, family, or financial success. Remember that success is spiritual metamorphosis.

Your decisions are yours and are your responsibility to God. Do not become a victim of limitations. Your ability to use your talents and your gifts will transcend the boundaries of mediocrity and self-pity, which often paralyze your ability to take action to take care of your family. What you achieve in life depends on the choices you make. Be mindful of the messages you send to your subconscious mind. Your subconscious mind functions like a tape recorder. It plays back what you program into it. "Finally, brethren whatsoever things are true, whatsoever things are noble, whatsoever things are just, whatsoever things are pure, whatsoever things are lovely, whatsoever things are of good report think on these things, if there be any virtue and if their be anything praiseworthy meditate on these things" (Philippians 4:8 NKJV).

Before I experienced and understood God's unconditional love and its effects on my life and the lives of my family members, I was like most young men—I wanted the thrill of new adventure. I left my job and hometown for the big city in search of pleasure and excitement. I went after it in hot pursuit—a passionate, aggressive search at a frantic pace in a risky and hazardous manner. First, it was motivation, then desperation, and finally frustration. I was desperately searching for pleasure and happiness. But the harder I tried, the more difficult it became. I finally came to the realization that the soul of man does not crave happiness, which is a momentary high that lifts him up and lets him down. The soul cries out for more than the happiness that comes from things and happenings. Deep down, I knew something was missing.

I was searching for something I had never seen or experienced. I was searching for that infinite power that supplies the gift of joyful living. I did not understand this until I was struck by reality. We have an infinite desire that reaches out for real joyful living. The hunger and thirst for joyful living is as real as the hunger and thirst for food and drink. We have the ability to satisfy our hunger and thirst, but we do not have the formula for real joyful living.

In our world today, people desperately search for happiness. They search for it in all the wrong places—by accumulating financial wealth, power, education, and marriage; as well as in stadiums, the theater, the ballpark, video stores, nightclubs, shopping malls, beaches, and drugstores; and with alcohol and illicit drugs and more. Millions of people suffer from mental depression and use drugs in an attempt to relieve symptoms of depression. We have become a pill-popping society. The essential factor needed to assimilate the formula for a joyful, caring, and loving marriage and family relationship is something that God alone can provide. He is the manufacturer, regulator, and dispenser of the formula for joyful living. Paul says, "Finally my brethren rejoice in the Lord" (Philippians 3:1 NKJV).

"Be anxious for nothing, by prayer and with thanksgiving let your requests be made known unto God, and the peace of God, which surpasses all comprehension, shall guard your hearts and minds in Christ Jesus" (Philippians 4:6–7 NKJV).

The question still remains: what is joyful living? Joyful living is contentment, serenity, and peace, which sustains cohesiveness and ecstasy when experiencing the unconditional love of God. In contrast to happiness, joyful living is the confident assurance that God's love in our lives will be there, no matter what! Happiness is an ingredient of joyful living, but joyful living is more than happiness. A person can be joyful, yet not show any outward sign of happiness. Everyone wants to be happy. Like Solomon, chasing after this elusive ideal becomes a lifelong passion, depleting our energy and time.

The Christian hope and faith provides us with confidence, knowing that when the feelings of happiness fade, we have the profound assurance of joyful living from knowing Christ personally. Build your marriage relationship on Christ's unconditional love, and you will experience real joyful living, no matter what.

There is a growing awareness in the field of psychoneuro-immunology (PNI) that deals with the connection between our emotions, nervous systems, and immune systems. Scientists now believe that something as intangible as emotion can trigger the production of regulatory chemicals that are carried throughout our minds and bodies, thus affecting life and health. Folded around the brain stem is our limbic system, which is composed of several interconnected structures. It is our brains' principal regulator of emotions. It influences the classification of memories that our brains store as long-term memories.

It also filters and interprets sophisticated incoming sensory information, in the context of our survival and emotional needs for joyful living.

Our Creator has designed us with all the potential factors our minds and bodies need to perform preventive maintenance and healing of the marriage and family relationship. Remember that our interests are shaped by our experiences, but our experiences can be shaped by our characters and lifestyles. Our desires are connected to our outlooks and the things we want to accomplish in this life. Desire is what connects us to the universal laws of nature, and it begins when we fully understand what we are trying to accomplish in life. The neurons and chemical reactions in our brains initiate actions and stimulate emotional reactions that control our behaviors.

The limbic system—the emotional clearinghouse of our minds and bodies—is the manufacturer, regulator, and dispenser of this powerful emotion that energizes joyful living. We may consciously or subconsciously follow the trail in search of joyful living, but how do we know when we have it? Let's complete our search for joyful marriages and family lifestyles by going back to the book of Philippians. The Philippian believers enjoyed a very special relationship with Paul. While he was in prison, he wrote them a personal letter of appreciation, expressing his love and affection for them.

This is how relationships become pillows of support for families and marriages when they are needed most. The concept of joy or rejoicing appears sixteen times in the book of Philippians and over 166 times in the Bible. This demonstrates the importance of joyful living—real joy in believing that a good lifestyle comes only from believing that Jesus paid it all, and through him comes eternal life. We will find joyful living through an unwavering belief in his blood, provided by his unconditional love. By believing that we are forgiven and believing that we are saved by grace, we must extend his forgiveness in our marriages and families. There is joyful living in serving unselfishly; joyful living in giving and giving thanks. Doing good to others should not be a duty but a joy. It is a joy, for it increases our own healthy and wealthy marriages from God's storehouse of love, which eliminates accumulated emotional deficits, such as high blood pressure, chronic fatigue syndrome, fibromyalgia, and other immune malfunctions and provides positive emotions that will allow us to enjoy our family relationships without being overly aggressive.

Our emotions are an integral part of our minds and bodies. They are designed and stored in a critical area of our brains for this purpose. Our emotions are conscious products of an unconscious process. Our emotions simply exist. We do not learn our emotions like we learn a subject, and we cannot easily change them—but they will easily change us. Emotions help us to respond quickly. They enhance health and wellness and have a good impact on families. Scientists are unlocking the mysteries of how our emotions, minds and bodies, health, and life itself are affected by a chronic negative attitude. Bill Moyers, in 1993, declared, that our emotions and our health are closely connected. This is not a new discovery. Our Creator/designer has emphasized this fact from the beginning of time. Our minds and bodies are the most magnificent specimens and architectural marvels that have been designed—phenomenal wonders that have scientists, biologists, health professionals, psychologists, researchers, and others devoting their lives to searching for answers.

They are desperately trying to find out why Christians and people who believe in prayer are more joyful, in better health, and heal faster when they are sick. They will never achieve this goal in their lifetimes, however, because the answer is not in science. This comes by faith and belief in God's creative power and the gift of his infinite love, which scientists are not willing to accept. This should allow us to develop a joyful assurance in our marriages and family lives as we continue our journeys, knowing that we are covered by God's abundant love and blessing.

Scientists now agree that negative responses do not differentiate between physical and emotional danger. What affects the emotions also affects our minds and bodies. We pay a high price for chronic negative emotional behavior. Cortisol and endorphins are peptide molecules that affect our daily lives. When our abilities to fend off danger triggers a negative response, cortisol, a kind of wonder drug, is released by our adrenal glands, which then activates important body/brain defense responses.

Low levels of cortisol produce the euphoria we need when we are in control, but sustained high levels are dangerous to our health and well-being. Endorphins, on the other hand, are a class of opiate peptides that modulate emotions within our pain/pleasure, stress/joy continuum. They reduce pain and negative attitudes and increase euphoria. Endorphin levels can be elevated by exercise and positive contacts with Christ, family, and friends. It is the resource of divine treasure that paves the pathway for unconditional love. The neurons of our brains are natural recording devices. We record on them the experiences that we are interested in, and we imbue those experiences with emotional meaning that we program by our lifestyles. Brain research shows that we actually grow more neurons or connection pathways that are associated with certain thinking and perception.

The things we focus on will influence our actions. It is said that a very large percentage of the things we think about daily are negative. We need to change those thought patterns, and nurture our brains with positive, joyful messages. "I can do all things through Christ who strengthens me" (Philippians

4:13 NKJV). Our perception of our marriage relationships will determine the success of our marriages and families.

Life begins with love, because the giver of life is love. In the beginning, God created the heavens and the earth. After the heavens were called into existence, the great God kneeled down, took a lump of clay, shaped it into his own image, and breathed his energy of life into his designed image, which became a living soul. Then, with the same gentle touch of love, he performed the first surgery. He took a rib from the man's side and made woman. God then performed the first marriage vow. What God has joined together should not be separated. As long as man and woman stay connected to the source of love, the healing energy of love will flow freely and abundantly, nurturing and sustaining family and life.

When all the cells, organs, and systems of our minds and bodies communicate and function efficiently, there is no need for negativity. Sin ruptured that connection, which resulted in sickness and death. Christ came and made provision for us to access and reconnect to the infinite power source of his divine love. The choice is yours. You can plug in to the receptacle of love or refuse to do it. Many psychologists and scientists have tried to discredit our Christian faith and belief in God's love and our desire to worship him. They have suggested that some genes influence people to worship. However, worship is a natural reaction, because we are created with the gift of worship by our Creator. We must remember that worship does not eliminate wholesome pleasure and laughter.

Learn to relax and enjoy real fellowship with friends, relatives, and family. Laughter is fun, inexpensive, and good medicine. Learn to laugh regularly. Tickle your limbic system with fun, and it will release life-giving health and invigorating chemicals into your mind and body. Laughter relaxes tense muscles; reduces blood pressure; exercises the muscles of the face, diaphragm, and abdomen; boosts the immune system; and releases pain-fighting hormones. Let your experience shape the foundation of a joyful marriage and family relationship and provide laughter and tranquility.

Laughter is better than massage and better than Valium or other medication. I can say this with confidence. After my surgery for prostate cancer, some friends visited me at the hospital. In our discussion, I mentioned that I had experienced excruciating pain whenever there was a desire to void my urine, which I could not do because a catheter was inserted. I joked, "I can understand what mothers-to-be experience when they have contractions in childbirth." My friend's wife suggested that whenever I experienced pain, I should take short breaths and breathe the way mothers do when they are in labor. We enjoyed the humor. After returning home, I was sitting in the living room when I felt the urge to void my urine. Without thinking, I rushed to the bathroom, and the pain started. It was intense, but I held on to the sink and started breathing as instructed by my friend's wife. While in that position, my cat, Mindy, came into the bathroom. She looked up at me with such an expression of sorrow and compassion, and she mewed, as if to say, "I am sorry for you!" Spontaneously, I started laughing, and in that moment of ecstasy, the pain went away. Sometimes what a sick person needs is a comedian, not a doctor. You can become your own comedian. Stand in front of the mirror and try to laugh. You will look so stupid that you will start laughing at yourself. There are times when married couples need fun and laughter in their lives, not professional marriage counseling.

How do we find joyful living? We find joyful living in service. We should be ready to serve our marriages and families, unselfishly and humbly. Service provides satisfaction and stimulates affection, which is a prerequisite for joyful living. "Let this mind be in you which was also in Christ Jesus" (Philippians 2:5 NKJV). We find joyful living in believing that we are created by God and believing that we are not alone in this journey of life. Believe that doing good for your family and others is a prerequisite for real joyful living. Believe that a giving commitment to marriage and family relieves stress. Joyful living comes when we give and when we give thanks to God. Always think of joy, for the mind is the remote control that turns on either dangerous levels of cortisol or life-giving fountains of contentment, serenity, and peace that elevates joyful living. God wants his people to be joyful, because he knows it has lasting benefits.

It all makes sense. The limbic system, the interconnection of emotions, the nervous system, the immune system and the body, cortisol, and endorphins are placed in our minds/bodies by God. These guarantee joy—real joy that is deeper than happiness, joy that sustains continuous and copious fountains of blessings. Joyful living surpasses euphoria; joyful living does not come from things or circumstances but from the love of Jesus. The love of Jesus is like an electromagnetic force that attracts kindness, meekness, compassion, and forgiveness. Every marriage and family needs joyful living to reestablish real family values. The limbic system is a collective term for a group of interconnected brain structures. These are involved in behaviors associated with survival, including: the expression of emotion, eating, drinking, defense, and reproduction, as well as the formation of memory. The key components of the limbic system are the hippocampus, amygdale, septal area, and the hypothalamus.

The hippocampus is located deep within the temporal lobe and is continuous with the cortex on the inner part of the lower surface of that lobe. It is also connected to other parts of the cerebral cortex, thalamus, and hypothalamus, which are essential in the formation of new memories. The amygdale is located in the temporal lobe, in front of the hippocampus. It is the link to the olfactory (small) system, hippocampus, and cerebral cortex and is an important center for expressions. These expressions are what make us special and unique.

Whenever you have a challenging day, remember that you are God's special creation, with special gifts and talents that can be used to provide for your needs. Do not allow yourself to become depressed with challenging, everyday work-related stress. We become overstressed when we worry about taking care of our families. It becomes a burden, and many marriages, families, and lives are destroyed. We have the ability to change our perceptions and the outcome of the things that affect our lives, negatively or positively. Many people try to drown their sorrows in alcohol, illicit drugs, or abusive behaviors.

We are to remember that Christ says, "Come to me, all you who labor and are heavy laden, and I will give you rest" (Matthew 11:28 NKJV).

The septal area, a small region of the inner surface of the brain, beneath the front of the corpus callosum, is linked to the hippocampus, amygdale, and hypothalamus. It is thought to be the pleasure or reward center. It is the focus of ongoing research in investigating addictive behavior.

The host of a popular, respected television show I was watching suggested there is evidence that one out of every ten Americans is addicted to drugs. I am not surprised, because almost every commercial break on TV promotes drugs—drugs for sexual enhancement, pain relief, weight loss, brain busters. There are drugs for everything.

Many seniors are surviving on drugs. When I was in the hospital, my roommate was taking many different drugs. The nurses were confused with the schedule. His daughter had to come to the ward and explain the purpose for the different drugs and his schedule. One day he told me that he sometimes felt as if he should stop taking the drugs and let nature determine his fate. It's not difficult to see why health care costs are so high. I was invited to take part in a men's health lecture, and one of the presenters gave information on natural remedies and suggested actions men can take to enhance their sex drive. These were all Christian men, but their response to the use of natural remedies lacked enthusiasm.

Another presenter from the public health department, who specialized in conventional medicine for impotence and other prostate problems, gave information on Viagra and other sex-enhancement drugs. The enthusiasm of the men was electrifying. Almost everyone asked questions and sought information on getting these drugs. They were not concerned about the side effects of the drugs, nor did they show any interest in natural remedies and lifestyle changes to allow the mind and body to provide the natural healing process.

Most of us are willing to take the easy way out. Your body is the temple of God, and in every phase of life, you should treat your body as a sacred vessel. Some of the chemicals we put into our minds and bodies make us more aggressive and impatient with our partners. We develop the lustful attitudes that are displayed on the TV screens and in some movies.

Some of us are trying to use synthetic man-made chemicals to replace the natural chemicals that our bodies produce for healing and optimum health and wellness. The hypothalamus is a tiny but vital region that regulates the activity of the body's organs (viscera) through connection of other parts of the brain that regulate the production of hormones. It is interconnected with parts of the limbic system and is responsible for bringing about changes associated with emotions, as well as cognitive changes from all mind and body interconnected structures. It is essential for the maintenance of the whole body.

The hypothalamus contains specialized receptor cells that can detect changes in the properties of circulating blood, such as temperature, hormone levels, and osmotic pressure. The hypothalamus is an important factor in the operation and maintenance of the whole body. It regulates hormone production in the pituitary gland and through neural connections with other parts of the brain and spinal cord. It provides overall control of the autonomic nervous system, which is known to coordinate activity in the body's internal organs.

It contains centers that regulate the heart and blood pressure, food intake, water balance, growth, and sexual reproduction. It is also important in the expression of emotions, such as fear, anger, and pleasure. The foods we eat and thoughts we think directly affect the performance of our minds and bodies. Thinking is a biochemical process that the brain cells use to communicate effectively with each other. The things we think about daily will create new neural pathways in our brains; these chemicals are known as neurotransmitters. The brain cells use neurotransmitters to carry messages from neuron to neuron. Neurotransmitters are made from amino acids found in protein foods. Vitamins and minerals are needed to convert ordinary amino acids into powerful neurotransmitters.

The three key neurotransmitters are acetylcholine, dopamine, and serotonin. It is suggested that acetylcholine neurotransmitter excites other neurons that may be responsible for memory. Dopamine generally excites other neurons and is involved in movement, attention, and learning. It is also involved with voluntary movement and emotional arousal. Serotonin is involved in sleep, mood, appetite, and sensitivity. It is excitatory and is part of the brain-reward system, providing feelings of natural pleasure. People who suffer from clinical depression may have too little serotonin activity in the synapses. These people could benefit from taking serotonin supplements. Serotonin-rich foods are carbohydrate-based foods, such as starchy vegetables, potatoes, cereals, grains, and fruits. Can you see why lifestyle is so important to optimum health and wellness and how it influences our actions and behaviors?

We are what we eat, what we drink, and what we think. Everything in our environment influences our lives, positively or negatively. In the journey of life, lifestyle also influences living standard, which in many ways is tied to the outcome of marriage and family. Many families are overstressed because of their hectic lifestyles.

The standard of living in any civilization is determined primarily by the extent to which people desire to influence their environments. The economy, the health care system, and the environment are influenced by our attitudes and actions. All of our services are dependent on how we value marriage, family, and society. Here are some examples: the goods and services we acquire for our use; the production and modification of our commodities; how we use the various manufacturing and processing of our food and other materials we have in our communities; scientific research; and much more—all these things are dependent on how we value marriage, family, and society. Modern technology has influenced our lifestyles to such a great extent that we allow ourselves to become dependent on others to think for us. The utilization of new technology for manufacturing and processing of commodities is tremendously important to our modern civilization. However, the manufacture of many of these highly complex products, which provide for our changing lifestyles and the desire for higher profits, has taken precedence over the health and well-being of our marriages, families, and society. Our Christian beliefs and family values and our moral standards are deteriorating. The effects can be seen in the escalation of broken marriages, broken homes, degenerative diseases, crime, war, and selfish gain, which are crippling our social, moral, and financial infrastructure.

The utilization of thousands of chemicals to preserve the shelf life of so many brands of processed foods also contributes to the ill health of many people. The growth hormones we add to our foods influence the behavior of society. Researchers and scientists have designed ways to produce genetically modified (GM) products that mimic the natural chemicals in our fruits, vegetables, and other whole foods.

These products are a quick fix and are deficient in the vital nutrients needed for our minds and bodies to acquire optimum health, which we need to develop healthy habits. Science and technology have made tremendous improvements in many areas of our society, and we need many of the advancements in our changing world, but we need to remember that in this journey of life, we cannot become complacent. Our goal is to reach the promised land of the physical, mental, spiritual, and emotional success of joyous living. This success will allow us to follow the divine pathway that our Creator mapped out for us—a pathway enlightened by Christian virtue and values.

Our visions, beliefs, and faith allow our neural pathways to convey messages of hope and joyful living. Researchers suggest that stress is a state of anxiety produced when events, responsibilities, and the choices we make exceed our capability to cope with the changing environment. We need to feed our minds with thoughts that provide contentment, serenity, and peace so that we can overcome negative emotional responses. We need to develop a positive consciousness of the importance of our health and the health of our marriages and family environments.

3

Power of Prayer

In our search for joyful living, we will attain our goals because with God, all things are possible, and "I [we] can do all things through Christ which strengtheneth me [us]" (Philippians 4:13 KJV). I have identified some of the actions we can take to keep our marriages and families together and build on our relationships every day as we continue the journey of life. In the beginning of this complex world, God looked at everything he had created and said, "It is very good." Then he looked at Adam. "And the Lord God said, 'It is not good that man should be alone; I will make him a helper comparable to him'" (Genesis 2:18 NKJV). The infinite God who created man in his own image declared that it is important for a man and a woman to have a special intimate relationship, one that is called marriage.

Christ has forgiven you, so before you make a decision, consult with him in prayer. Prayer is power. It can reconnect you to the source of energy and allow currents of divine love to flow, recharge your dead batteries, and reenergize your relationships.

If you do not learn to relax and believe that success is possible, you will not succeed, and you will doom yourself to failure before you begin your journey. With a spiritually healthy and wealthy mind, prayer can make a difference in your attitude.

How you approach your journey in life and deal with difficult or challenging situations sends a message to others who are following in the path you have traveled. Let your message be positive and encouraging.

I have learned that experience, along with training, is the best way to success. When we take appropriate actions to plan and build a solid foundation to support our marriages and families, the wind and storm will come, but the foundation of our prayer lives will keep the building firm and secure on the solid rock, Jesus Christ.

When two people start a partnership to search for their buried treasure of a successful family life, they must design a plan and a "feasibility study" on the cost of building the project, and extract, develop, and refine their values of joyful living, which are essential to marriage and family. My recommendation for a feasibility study is prayer and God's designed plan, given to us from the beginning of creation and printed in his sacred manual, the Bible.

When we use the plan Christ has given to us, we build beautiful family relationships that last for eternity. As we continue our search for joyful living, let us take some advice from Paul. "And this I pray, that your love may abound still more and more in knowledge and all discernment, that you may approve the things that are excellent, that you may be sincere and without offence till the day of Christ" (Philippians 1:9–10 NKJV). Statistics have shown that many marriages fail because couples do not take the appropriate actions to save their marriages and families. I know from experience that construction companies take appropriate action to protect their business, workers, and work environment. This allows them to improve production and profit. For marriage to be successful, wives and husbands must be willing to implement new and creative strategies to protect their marriages, their children, and their family environments. This formula will build, expand, and improve their relationships.

Everyone who seeks improvement in this special union—marriage—needs to make decisions and take action to nurture that relationship in order to have a productive family value. A small investment returns a small production and profit; a large investment returns a large production and profit. What value do you place on your marriage and family? As for me, my marriage is priceless. My marriage has saved my life. Many of the young men that I saw as my role models before I changed my lifestyle now are dead. I learned that one of the men, who had been most popular with the ladies and who had cheated on many women and had many kids with different women, shot his second wife and then shot himself because she left him. This could have been me, if it was not for Christ, the power of prayer, and my wife, lover, and friend. She was my support base when I went through episodes of illness, including cancer. Her tender loving care and encouragement lifted my spirit and prayer life and gave me strength to endure.

Wives and husbands should make every challenging moment of their life journeys a learning experience. They should develop a willingness to learn and accept new ideas that will enhance healthy relationships. Some couples allow negative and stressful work environments to affect their marriages and families. It is imperative that husbands and wives avoid bringing home an unpleasant experience from work. This will disrupt their family environments and lead to serious incidents. I have personal experience in bringing a challenging workday home. I went home feeling stressed, became angry with my wife and children, and was not in an approachable mood. I was not physically or verbally abusive, but body language says a lot.

Do not get me wrong; sometimes family is the best support base. When you have a difficult day at work, they are there to comfort and support you. Always believe in your family and in your spouse; they are your special cheerleaders. I am so thankful that I have a compassionate and understanding wife who takes action to defuse time bombs before they go off. When I make mistakes by saying the wrong thing, she may be angry, but she knows when to be calm and serene, because she knows that we all have challenging days. She always provides a shoulder to lean on.

Learning is a continuous process. We must use our experiences to develop a mental attitude and conscious awareness of unsafe environments—mentally, physically, and emotionally. Unsafe attitudes, words, or actions will cause incidents that could be fatal to our marriages and families and could "short circuit" our energy to support joyful living. A strong belief in Christ and a prayer base will guide us in our search for joyful relationships that will continue until death.

A hazardous emergency in marriage could happen to anyone at anyplace, anywhere, or at any time. Such a situation demands your undivided attention and an awareness of the danger on your journey of life. When you are confronted with a hazardous experience, the power of prayer will never fail, so use it regularly, and let it be your essential tool for survival.

Believe that all things are possible with Christ as your guiding light—he shines brightly to guide your path. Use your Christ-given virtues, experience, and training to overcome challenges as you navigate any hostile terrain of family life. Pray for Christ's grace to enlighten your journey, which will lead to a successful life filled with joyful living, contentment, and peace. Christ-awareness will allow you to maintain and overcome incredible odds and will give you added incentive to be a successful wife or husband.

Successful living is your ability to accomplish your goal, regardless of the difficulties you experience in your everyday challenging activities. To be successful is to believe in a healthy and prayer-filled marriage and family life that is alive and well, in an environment where lifestyle is more important than our sacred vows. My personal experience of prayer teaches me that to have a successful marriage we need to accept challenges, and use them as learning experience. This action gives me the ability to develop mental, physical and spiritual strength to enjoy marriage and family in good times and some not-so-good times.

These experiences will also enhance our ability to assess other hazardous terrain along life's highway. Success in achievement largely depends on your state of mind, for what the mind perceives, the mind can achieve. You and I can do all things through the power of prayer, which strengthens us, if we truly believe and take relevant action with the success formula of daily prayer and worship. We will achieve prayer-oriented, joyful, successful, and prosperous family lives.

The healthier our self-awareness and self-esteem, the more inclined we are to take action that will enhance our abilities to achieve our objectives of healthy, wealthy, and joyful marriages and family lives—financially, physically, mentally, spiritually, and emotionally balanced. The positive action we take will allow us to face the difficult challenges we will encounter. Our prayer lives will pave our pathways and take us to our destinations of real success.

Remember that your brain is one of the most valuable pieces of equipment that God has given you. If you use it with confidence, there is no limit to true success. The most physically well-equipped people are not always those who are the most successful in handling hazardous emergency situations. Married couples and families, who use their knowledge and the direction of God's words as their guiding lights also are successful. Love for others and the power of prayer will help us to develop confidence, and belief in God will eliminate or contain the hazardous conditions we encounter and give us the tenacity to "keep on keeping on," no matter what. Several challenges could have derailed my and Theresa's marriage, but we learned early in our journey that we all have faults, and we made allowances to balance our differences.

Let me reemphasize that there are no perfect couples. Our key for success is prayer. Prayer allows us to take action to defuse or eliminate a confrontation. I can vividly remember an incident in Jamaica. We had a male quartet at our church. I would take them to singing engagements, along with a young lady who was a soloist and sometimes sang with the quartet. A young woman, whose husband was part of the quartet, once approached my wife and asked her why she allowed this soloist to travel in my car.

Theresa assured the young woman that the five men in the car were doing God's ministry, but this young wife was not comfortable with her husband's traveling in the car with the female soloist; she felt insecure. Theresa felt secure because she had trust and confidence in herself and our relationship. In our life journeys, we have to believe in our partners and trust in each other. When there is doubt, talk to God in prayer. Theresa's and my relationship was established by prayer, and by grace, we will continue our journey by faith with prayer. "And whatever things you ask in prayer, believing you will receive" (Matthew 21:22 NKJV).

You will encounter many hazards in your journey. Take time to mentally assess and evaluate the situations; do not become fearful or anxious. Your attitude will affect your good judgment. You are given the ability to adapt, live, and work in stressful environments. Families, married couples, and those who are planning to get married must use their God-given abilities to adapt to stressful environments and be willing to endure some of the difficulties that are associated with challenging environments. In the work environment, people may quit their jobs when they experience challenging conditions. Others cannot depend on them. These people always see something to complain about and suggest why the project must be shut down. In marriages and in families, we experience similar problems. "But without faith it is impossible to please him; for he that cometh to God must believe that he is, and that he is the rewarded of them that diligently seek him" (Hebrews 11:6 KJV).

In sports, there are "fair-weather fans." These are the people who support the team only when the team is doing well. These fans bail at the first sign of trouble and start cheering for another team that seems to be doing better. Some marriages, too, will survive only in comfortable conditions. Too many of us are fair-weather spouses. These husbands and wives are willing to sacrifice their marriages and their families for another family that seems to be doing better. When things do not work out, they then want to go back to the wives or husbands they have abandoned. They are not established on the foundation of God's love and the instruction given by Paul: "Wives submit to your own husbands, as to the Lord. For the husband is the head of the wife, as also Christ is head of the church; and he is the Savior of the body. Husbands, love your wives just as Christ also loved the church and gave himself for her" (Colossians 3:18–21 NKJV). Sometimes marriages go through times of stress, struggle, or trial. But remember when you were in love, and things were wonderful? You were your spouse's biggest cheerleader. Even in times of stress, struggle, and trial, your spouse and your marriage needs you to continue cheering. Your marriage is worth working for, even when it is not what you want it to be. When the "weather conditions" of your marriage turn cold, remember that spring is coming, and after spring there is summer. It is worth the wait.

Your ability to remain dedicated and committed to your marriage—even in hard times—will carry your marriage through. "He who does not love does not know God, because God is love" (1 John 4:8 NKJV).

In our journey of life, there are no guarantees. The weather conditions can change without any warning; we must travel with a survival kit—our faith in Jesus Christ's love. We have been given the gifts of love and compassion by our Creator, to be of service to our families and all people. Use these gifts well. Take time to develop a positive mental attitude of love and work with your partner.

With prayer, you can develop confidence in your ability to succeed. When we claim God's promises, we must step out in faith. "For everyone who asks receives, and he who seeks finds, and to him who knocks it will be open" (Matthew 7:8 NKJV). Remember, you have made a commitment to your partner and to God. Do not take it lightly. Use your experience to help others achieve success in their goals and objectives, and you will be rewarded with additional gifts and talents of unique qualities that will strengthen your marriage and family.

By helping others, you help yourself. Knowledge is potential power; it is only useful when put into service. When you use it, you will gain more. You must be willing, by God's grace, to visualize a picture in your mind, and use your God-given knowledge to guide your path. Prayer is power; it will energize your marriage and relationships and sustain joyful living. With God, everything is possible. All things work together for good to those who believe and take positive action to complete their tasks. "And we know that all things work together for good to those who love God, to those who are the called according to his purpose" (Romans 8:28 NKJV).

Attitude is a state of mind that influences your actions and reactions to life's challenges. Your attitudes and actions are the most important ingredients of a successful marriage and family life. With the proper attitude, everything is possible. To make it through life successfully, the right attitudes and actions are imperative and powerful tools. Entertain a willingness to help your family achieve goals and objectives.

Our minds have the potential power to influence and guide our thoughts and attitudes to accomplish phenomenal and extraordinary goals, even those we did not believe possible. Research has shown that taking the right action is often a major factor for success. If married couples and families take appropriate action for a successful journey, there will be less illness, crime, and social problems. In our relationships with one another, we must have the same mind-set and attitude as Christ Jesus. "Let this mind be in you which was also in Christ Jesus" (Philippians 2:5 NKJV).

Many people ask Theresa and me for the secret to our fifty years of successful marriage. It is prayer, love, and commitment to each other and God. We have invested our time and talents, because our marriage and family depends on our success. With opportunity provided by prayer and belief in God, we can develop our mental skills and abilities so that we can challenge any hazardous conditions and make possible whatever seems to be impossible for our family.

A successfully outcome is possible in all challenging situations, but it demands that marriage partners and families have a personal willingness to develop an attitude of cooperation and unity. Always visualize that your marriage can withstand any challenge you encounter. "Be anxious for nothing, but in everything by prayer and supplication, with thanksgiving, let your request be made known to God" (Philippians 4:6 NKJV).

From my experience on construction sites, I have learned that workers can be very brave and resourceful in emergency situations. The most important factor for a successful marriage and family life, however, is to prevent and eliminate the hazards *before* they become emergencies. We should always evaluate our personal environment for mental and physical hazards to our marriages and families. There is no magic formula. Real success is achieved by commitment to our marriages, our families, and God, by using his policy and procedures. "You will keep him in perfect peace, whose mind is stayed on you, trust in the Lord forever, for in Yah, the Lord, is everlasting strength" (Isaiah 26:3 NKJV).

Your mind cooperates with your body to control your thoughts, attitudes, and actions. A stressful environment will challenge your ability to succeed when the going gets difficult. What affects you mentally will affect you physically and emotionally; therefore, you must use the power of prayer to develop mental and spiritual attitudes that appreciate the success of others. If you think that you are more important than others, you will become a liability to your marriage, family, and community. Your goals and objectives demand your commitment and responsibility to your family and community.

A research paper on prayer for partners reported the results of five studies. Reviewed by John M. Grohol, PsyD, on May 16, 2013, it was designed to find out whether partner-focused prayer shifted individuals toward cooperative behavior, both over time and in the immediate aftermath of hurtful behavior. Study participants were undergraduate college students who indicated they were comfortable with prayer and praying for others.

Among the findings are the following points:

- Participants who prayed more frequently for their partners were rated as less vengeful in discussing something those partners had done to upset or annoy them.
- The partners of participants who prayed for them noticed more forgiving behavior than the partners of participants who were assigned to set aside time each day to think positive thoughts about them.
- Participants assigned to pray following partners' hurtful behavior were more cooperative with their partners, as compared to participants assigned to engage in thinking about God.
- Participants who prayed for a close relationship with partners on days in which conflict occurred reported higher levels of cooperative tendencies and forgiveness than on days when conflict occurred and they did not pray.

When we focus on ourselves, we lose the bigger picture. The above research information demonstrates that we need to be more sensitive to the needs of others and to develop a forgiving spirit that will heal our hearts and minds.

"These findings highlight the potential benefit of using partner-focused prayer were culturally appropriate, in clinical settings or in relationship education programs," the researchers wrote. In addition to informing relationship education and couples, they prayed for religious clients. The research findings may also help clarify the types of interventions, such as those that increase cooperation in order to facilitate forgiveness, which might be developed for nonreligious couples, according to the researchers.

The primary reason to focus on the role of prayer in healing is not to prove its effectiveness scientifically - although this can be done, I feel and is one of the tasks of this book. The best reason goes deeper: Prayer says something incalculably important about who we are and what our destiny may be. As we shall see, prayer is a genuinely nonlocal event - that is, not confined to a specific place in space or to a specific moment in time. *(Dossey 1993)*

My personal experience in the power prayer provides physical, mental, and spiritual healing in sickness and in marriage. This make me a true believer in making prayer an important factor of daily life. It will improve your trust and belief in marriage and family. "God is interested in all that concerns us and we come to him even with what may seem trivial matters. That he asks us to come is in itself significant, for we cannot believe that God would invite us if all he had in mind was to ignore our plea" (Andreasen 1957). He will never forsake us, his banner over us is love.

4

Sex Heals, Sex Kills

I've mentioned that sex is a precious blessing given to us by God. It increases the blessing of a real relationship between a wife and husband. Many people in the world use the word *sex* loosely, and many Christians are uncomfortable using it at all. Words that relate to sex become "bad" or distasteful when they are used to discredit someone's integrity or are used for cursing. I feel this devalues the meaning of sex. When married couples intentionally develop a real sexual relationship in their marriage, however, amazing changes happen in their lives. For example:

> Hugging increases levels of "love hormone," oxytocin. This, in turn may have beneficial effects on your heart, health and more. One study found, for instance, that women had lower blood pressure following a brief episode of warm contact with their partner. A 20-second hug, along with 10 minutes of hand-holding, also reduces the harmful physical effects of stress, including its impact on your blood pressure and heart rate. *(Mercoa.com, Mercola)*.

"The hormone oxytocin, which is known to be important in trust, may also be involved in a sense of well-being. According to new research, women who show large increases in oxytocin when they are trusted also report being more satisfied with life and less depressed" *(Science Daily 2010).*

Wives and husbands have seen their marriages go from bad to good and from good to great when they become more intimate. Sex is much more than physical interaction. It becomes therapeutic when both partners understand that they are one in body. It is an intimate relationship that is established to produce a nuclear family. Some researchers say that no matter where your marriage is, ten days of sexual intimacy will draw you closer together. But what happens when one partner experiences a low sex drive because of medical or biological challenges? From my personal experience, sex is wonderful, but it should not be the foundation of a marriage. The foundation of a marriage should be love and trust built on God's unconditional love.

When it comes to frequency of sex, science says "just do it." More and more studies show increased emotional and physical benefits from frequent safe sex. Some of the benefits they suggested are that it can ease a headache, lower mortality rates, reduce risk of prostate cancer, improve posture, and boost self-esteem. Sex makes a person feel younger, helps prevent yeast infections, and offers pain relief, including pain from migraines and back pain. It gives people a positive attitude on life, makes a person calmer, makes skin healthier, and improves a person's fitness level. Having sex makes a person less irritable, and it reduces depression. Sex improves the sense of smell and has a therapeutic effect on the immune system. It helps bladder control. It relieves stress and menstrual cramps and helps people sleep better. It improves digestion and increases circulation. Sex helps improve the ability to produce chemicals in the brain to stimulate the growth of new dendrites (extension of nerve cells).

Sex lowers the level of cortisol, a hormone that can trigger fatigue and cravings; lowers feelings of insecurity; improves pelvic muscle tone; increases levels of commitment; leads to less frequent colds and flu; and improves vaginal tissue lubrication. It can help people achieve weight loss, since about two hundred calories are burned during thirty minutes of active sex. Studies show that it is a myth that abstinence can sharpen a person's competitive edge. I will not disagree with these studies. My question, however, is, what is safe sex? The study did not include any information on married couples. The study also suggested that when partners in a long-term committed relationship hit a point where there is an obvious difference in sex drives, any difficulties in talking about sex can quickly become magnified. While you may have tried to talk about the issue on several occasions, it can quickly feel like something neither of you wants to talk about.

At that point, talking may not be the best thing to do, but eventually, you have to start communicating about the issue in order to get through it—or even end the relationship in a respectful and loving way. Here are some ideas on what to do when talking isn't working anymore. This report on sex demonstrates why marriages are failing. There is no doubt that sex is wonderful and helps to improve marriage, but a marriage relationship is very weak if it is built just on sex. When a man and woman are joined together, they become one flesh. "So then they are no longer two but one flesh. Therefore what God joined together, let not man separate" (Matthew 19:6 NKJV). This gives them the sacred right to intimacy, love, and sex to build and improve their relationship.

My wife and I enjoy an excellent relationship. For us, sex is just one of the important ingredients in our marriage relationship. A real sex life starts long before the wife and husband enter the bedroom. Wives and husbands must enjoy being together. Sharing moments of walking together, working together, worshipping together will help couples to be one in mind and spirit. In today's lifestyle, sex has become cheap; it often is based on the exploitation of women. Men and women degrade sex to just a physical encounter. There are many sex crimes, including women being sold as sex slaves and sexual abuse. Many lives are disrupted because of sex. Many people's lives are lost because of sex. AIDS has robbed many people of their lives. So-called lovers kill their sex partners.

Sex is not the problem. It is the uncontrolled lust for sex that controls and destroys many people's lives. Some husbands and wives cheat on each other because of lust. In everything, we must be temperate; anything that controls our actions can become dangerous to our health. When sex is based on just intercourse, it is more dangerous to our health and to the health and safety of families.

Just by breathing and metabolizing food, our body creates what are known as free radicals. Free radicals are molecules with unpaired electrons. These unstable molecules make their way through our bodies, scavenging our cells, trying to snatch up the missing parts. Some researchers suggest that the damage that free radicals do to our cells could be the reason why our minds and bodies age and die. When we are young, our cells have a defense system, known as superoxide dismutase (SOD), that controls the free radicals, but as we grow older, SOD does not work effectively. This allows the free radicals to have their way with our cells, and when the damage gets to be too much, the cells become diseased and die—and so do we. Free radicals have been implicated in a number of illnesses and diseases, which become more frequent as we age.

This awful, disruptive condition could be used to explain the unstable behavior of our marriages and families. Some men and women behave like free radicals, roaming our communities, snatching wives or husbands from their partners, damaging and destroying vulnerable marriages and families. When wives and husbands are newly married, their new romantic attraction is their "defense" system, defending against "marital free radicals." As some married relationships grow older, the sentimental attraction and tender loving care becomes weak and does not work effectively. This allows marital free radicals to have their way with marriages and families. The damage can have a domino effect for some marriages and families, and they experience one episode of illness after another until the death of their marriages, families, and family values. Antioxidants are used to contain and eliminate free radicals in the human body. I believe unconditional love can be used to contain and eliminate "marital free radicals" in our communities. One of the Greek root words for love is *eros*—love of passion. The English word erratic is taken from the same root word for eros (*erot*). Many marriages fall apart because they are controlled by passion and erratic behavior—unpredictable, fluctuating—which does not instill confidence. Marriage and family relationships need *agape* to provide a strong foundation of support and to elevate eros to a meaningful, acceptable standard that is suitable for wife and husband.

When my wife and I started having children, I became jealous when she gave more attention to my son and daughter than to me. It took some time for me to understand that children are a blessing to improve our family and our relationship and to sustain joyful living. In the journey of life, wives and husbands are supposed to grow old together, enjoying each other's touch and romantic affection. My wife and I went to Riu Ocho Rios to celebrate our fiftieth anniversary; it was exciting. We enjoyed the facilities at the resort, walking together, sitting on the beach together, and going on tours together. Everything was therapeutic. When we went to church on the first Sabbath, the church was celebrating Family Day, and we became the special family. The following Sabbath, we went to the church where we were baptized and married. We were welcomed with enthusiasm, and we were honored and elated. The Rollington Town SDA Church brought back welcome memories and made us feel blessed. These precious memories filled us with joy and encouraged us to keep on keeping on until Christ calls us home. The following week, we went to Morant Bay SDA Church. I was asked to give a presentation on love, courtship, and marriage.

The experiences we had fellowshipping with our church family are wonderful blessings that money cannot buy. They are our precious treasures that will elevate marriage and family. My presentation used my personal experience and encounters with Christ, his church, and the gift of my wife. These are the moments that bring us abundant joy—to share our experiences with others. Love is much more than sex. Sex provides complete intimate love that makes the wife and husband's relationship different from what the world experiences.

Studies have shown that women may not be the only ones who suffer the effects of changing hormones. Doctors have noticed that men are reporting some of the same symptoms that women experience in menopause. Doctors say that male patients who received hormone therapy with testosterone reported relief from some of the symptoms associated with so-called male menopause. Because men do not go through a well-defined period referred to as menopause, doctors refer to this problem as *andropause* (testosterone) decline in the aging male, or what some people call low testosterone.

Men do experience a decline in the production of the male hormone testosterone with aging, but this also occurs with conditions such as diabetes. Along with the decline in testosterone, some men experience symptoms that include fatigue, weakness, depression, and sexual problems. When men reach their late forties to early fifties, some may experience a reduction in libido (sex drive), erectile dysfunction, weight gain, fatigue, depression, and other emotional symptoms, which bear some similarities to symptoms of female menopause. Men should be aware of this condition, because some men place blame for their low sex drive on their wives, and they then experiment with younger women. I have listened to men discuss their sex lives on construction sites, as well as in some social gatherings (where you would not expect to hear such talk). Many of them believe that younger women are the answer to their sex problems, but others turn to enhancement drugs. Stress, illness, and other emotional factors also contribute to low sex drive. Wives should be educated on male sexual problems. Communication in marriage is very important in order to sustain a meaningful relationship. Some men are sensitive about their low sex drive and are likely to abstain from sex, which will send the wrong message to their wives—some wives may believe their husbands are cheating on them. One man told me that after his surgery for prostate cancer, he was impotent. He went into depression for eighteen months. There are critical times in married relationships when sex is not the answer. When wives and husbands face difficult times, they need each other's support.

Research suggests that the number of middle-aged men with prescriptions for testosterone is climbing rapidly, raising concerns that increasing numbers of men are abusing the powerful hormone to boost their libidos to feel younger.

> Testosterone replacement therapy is approved specifically for the treatment of abnormal low testosterone levels, a condition called hypogonadism. The hormone helps build muscle, reduce body fat and improve sex drive. But a study published in the journal JAMA Internal Medicine found that many men who get prescriptions for the hormone have no evidence of a deficiency at all. *(New York Times 2013).*

The emotions and attitudes toward life are likely to change in the direction of boredom, restlessness, feelings of stagnation, and depression. For many of us, stress and anxiety have become so much a part of our daily experiences that we fail to notice the harmful effects. It can build up gradually over days, weeks, and months until eventually, we recognize symptoms of emotional or behavioral disturbance. These are times when we need tender loving care. When I was diagnosed with prostate cancer, I felt blessed to have Theresa as my wife. She was there for me every step of the way—for better or for worse, until death do we part. Her actions demonstrated her love and caring spirit and devotion.

Exercise is often more productive for a low sex drive than most drugs. Here are some foods suggested on Health.com (October 16, 2011) for assisting sex enhancement.

- Avocados are rich in heart-healthy fats, and anything that keeps your heart beating strong will help to keep blood flowing to all the right places.
- Almonds are nutrient-dense and rich in trace minerals, such as zinc, selenium, and vitamin E, which are important for sexual health and reproduction.
- Strawberries are an excellent source of folic acid (vitamin B-9), which helps to ward off birth defects and may also be effective in producing a higher sperm count.
- Some seafood, such as salmon, contains heart-healthy omega-3 fats. Those of us who are vegetarians should substitute other sources of omega-3 fats.
- Arugula contains trace minerals and antioxidants that block absorption of environmental contaminants, which could negatively affect your libido.
- Figs contain fiber, which is important for heart health.
- Citrus fruits are rich in antioxidants, vitamin C, and folic acid, which are essential for men's reproductive health.

Men and women with a reduced sex drive could try these natural foods. They do not have negative effects on your mind or body.

5

Value of Exercise

Exercise is an essential factor to enhance healthy and wealthy marriages and family lifestyle. It precipitates the ability to function efficiently at home and work and helps to eliminate physical, mental, and emotional fatigue that could cause injury to healthy relationships. Neuromotor exercise, recommended by the American College of Sport Medicine, will help wives and husbands prevent physical and spiritual falls, help with muscle dystrophy, and energize the mind and body. Growing evidence and research indicates that exercise triggers genes and growth factors that will energize and rejuvenate the brain cells, muscle, and tissues that are important for optimal health.

These growth factors include muscle regulatory factors. Growth factors are local regulators that are produced by our anterior pituitary glands. They are modified fatty acids that stimulate bone and cartilage growth. Research information shows that they are located on the surface of cancer cells and stimulate abnormal cell division. They are proteins that bind to cell-surface receptors that stimulate growth and development of target cells.

Target cells are specific cells that respond to a specific hormone. Target cells have special receptors on their outer membranes that allow the individual hormones to bind to the cell. Our minds and bodies are composed of a variety of different hormones, including growth and sex hormones, which carry messages between our organs and cells. Hormones are secreted by glands in the endocrine system to help the body stay balanced and to function optimally. The main sex hormones include estrogen, progesterone, testosterone, pregnenolone, and DHEA. The aging process is associated with loss of sex hormones in both men and women. Exercise will help to replace those lost hormones and can restore feelings of well-being, sex drive and sexual pleasure, and energy levels, as well as reverse muscle and bone loss, along with other functions that are associated with aging. In my estimation, a healthy and wealthy marriage supersedes physical and material gain. It is a balance lifestyle that promotes joyful living.

By exercising, you can age more slowly and gracefully and have a better quality of life and a natural sex drive. Health and wealth are dynamic processes because they are always changing. We all have times of good health and times of sickness. As your life changes, so does the level of your health and wellness. The mind, body, and spirit provide balance to enhance the quality of life. Anabolic hormones are crucial to our health and wellness; they influence positive lifestyles. Hormones and receptors fit together much like a lock and key. Most hormones circulate in the blood, coming into contact with essentially all the cells. Human growth hormones are powerful anabolic hormones that occur naturally in our bodies. They are produced by the pituitary gland in the brain and stimulate growth of muscle, cartilage, and bones and are made throughout a person's lifetime. Your entire body is designed to produce growth hormones when they are needed for their special task. Adding growth hormone to your diet in the form of steroids or taking sexual enhancement drugs will complicate the work of growth hormones and reduce the ability of your mind and body to function efficiently and empower your self-esteem and self-confidence in marriage and family relationships.

Growth hormone stimulates growth in children and plays an important role in adult metabolism. Scientists first isolated human growth hormone, or HGH, in 1956, and three years later, National Health Service (NHS) doctors began to use it in the treatment of children suffering from stunted growth. Research also suggested that before the advent of genetic engineering, the only known source of HGH was in human corpses. It is also suggested that the pituitary glands were removed from cadavers, processed, and made available in injectable form. In our advanced technological society; synthetic HGH can be made in unlimited quantities in the laboratory, and many people are using it for performance. Its use in sports was banned in 1989 by the International Olympic Committee's medical commission; according to the BBC News.

Exercise helps our bodies to produce natural human growth hormones. As we grow older, our growth production slows down. Adults are encouraged to exercise daily to enhance their production of growth hormones. Growth hormones act on the liver to increase blood sugar levels in our bloodstream. They act on muscles to increase lean body mass, which we need as we go into our golden years. They also act on fat cells to reduce their size and increase free-floating fat to improve our energy. The energizing force for every organ in our bodies comes from our brains.

Wives and husbands whose occupations require them to sit or stand continuously are less able to get blood to their brain tissues because their tired organs find it difficult to force blood to ascend against the force of gravity. If our brain tissues are denied adequate blood, eventually every organ in our bodies will suffer; therefore, exercise is important to optimal health and work performance. Human growth hormone is designed by our Creator to turn on other growth factors that increase organ size and bone length. We are fearfully and wonderfully made. Using synthetic HGH can be dangerous for our health.

Regular and adequate exercise will provide balance to our normal HGH.

Preventive maintenance of our minds and bodies is our responsibility. As we get to the twilight of our lives, our bodies produce less growth hormone, because we are no longer growing and do not have the need to generate as many new cells on a regular basis, as the body normally does when we are younger. These growth factors signal brain stem cells and muscle stem cells, which are found in our skeletal muscle fibers and promote growth, repair, and regeneration, to convert them into new neurons and new muscle cells. Adults can also become deficient in growth hormone. This will affect the ability to perform to normal standards at home and work.

Brain-derived neurotrophic factor (BDNF) acts on certain neurons of the central nervous system and the peripheral nervous system to help support the survival of existing neurons and support their growth and differentiate new neurons and synapses. In our brains, BDNF is active in the hippocampus, cortex, and basal forebrain.

> BDNF also expresses itself in the neuromuscular system where it protects motor neurons from degradation. BDNF's activity in both the muscles and the brain appear to be major part of the explanation for why a physical workout can have such a beneficial impact BDNF also expresses itself in the neuromuscular system where it protects motor neurons from degradation. BDNF's activity in both the muscles and brain appear to be a major part of the explanation for why a physical workout can have such beneficial impact on brain tissues. *(Canadian Foundation for Trauma Research & Education 2011)*

This is why physical workouts are beneficial to brain tissue and organs. Exercise helps prevent brain atrophy and age-related muscle degeneration. My wife and I make exercise an important part of our lifestyle. Research shows that exercise can increase the brain chemical epinephrine, which has a significant impact on memory and is found in higher levels after exercise. It also suggests that exercise may slow the effects of Alzheimer's disease, and brain structure is boosted when people live an active lifestyle. Research also found that maintaining an active lifestyle is important for an optimally healthy mind and body.

The areas of the brain that benefit from an active lifestyle are those that consume the most energy, and they are very sensitive to damage. The more active your lifestyle, the healthier your mind and body are likely to be. The general rule, in physical exercise training, is that as soon as an exercise becomes easy to complete, we need to increase the intensity and/or try another exercise to keep challenging our minds and bodies.

Our trainer recommends high-intensity interval (anaerobic) training, in which we alternate short bursts of high-intensity exercise with gentle recovery periods. My study manual, *Foundations of Professional Personal Training*, suggests that it is important that we do not exercise the same muscle groups every day. Our bodies have twenty-nine core muscles, located mostly in the back, abdomen, and pelvis. This special group of muscles provides the foundation for movement throughout the entire body. Strengthening these muscles can help protect and support the back, make the spine and body less prone to injury, and help us gain the greater balance and stability we need to perform daily tasks. When I worked on a construction site in the oil and sand industry, workers were encouraged to stretch in the morning before starting daily tasks. Stretching works with the body's natural physiological makeup to improve circulation and increase the elasticity of muscle joints. Stretching also allows the body to repair itself.

Foundation exercises, developed by Dr. Eric Goodman, are all about your core. Dr. Goodman explains that the core is anything that connects to the pelvis, including hamstrings, glutes, and adductor muscles. Foundation training is a special form of exercise that teaches all your muscles to work together through integrated chains of movement—which is how we are structurally designed by our Creator to move—as opposed to isolated movements, like crunches. Foundation training is recommended by many professional trainers, as it can address the root cause of lower back pain, which is related to weakness and imbalance among the posterior chain of muscles. Many of us have bad posture. Standing for long periods places pressure on the lower back. You should practice a hanging position, a technique practiced in foundation exercises, and also stretch regularly.

These muscle imbalances also may be related to lengthy sitting. Anyone who spends long hours sitting in front of a computer or at a desk should take a micro-break and do deep breathing and stretching. Exercise can be used to improve posture, range of motion, and the functionality. It can help treat the underlying cause of pain, as well as help prevent chronic neck pain from developing.

Exercise helps prevent and relieve pain through a number of mechanisms, such as strengthening key supportive muscles, and it also helps to restore flexibility. Studies have shown that repetitive strain injuries have become increasingly common because many office workers spend most of their workdays sitting in front of computers, and after work they spend time watching TV.

Computer work, to a great extent, is associated with neck pain, specifically originating from the trapezius muscle. Many types of neck pain are caused by long hours of sitting with poor posture. I have experienced neck pain from long hours of typing on the computer. Prolonged sitting also can make our posture even worse. For instance, one study by the *Clinical Journal of Pain* showed that people with chronic neck pain demonstrate a reduced ability to maintain an upright posture. The same study further shows that people who followed a specific exercise program experienced an improved ability to maintain a neutral cervical posture during prolonged sitting, which suggests that exercise should be introduced in the working community to help break the poor posture/neck pain cycle.

Other research has similarly shown that exercise is incredibly beneficial for treating neck pain. Body growth and repair occurs only during rest or sleep, never during exercise. Successful development of your body requires a delicate balance of a proper exercise program and the correct raw materials from your food, such as vitamins, minerals, and antioxidants, as well as rest and sleep to maintain and repair damaged tissue, build new tissue, and allow new growth to take place. The body becomes overtaxed and stressed when it does not get sufficient rest.

As we get older, many of us as become overly stressed because of aches and pains, and many of those problems are caused by lack of exercise. You do not have to go to the gym to exercise. Wives and husbands can go on leisurely walks regularly, which also will allow them to enjoy nature and improve their relationship. I have discovered that many seniors are getting divorced or are separating from their spouses. Sitting on the couch, watching television, decreases communication and also may lead to weight gain. Weight gain sometimes leads to depression and stressors, which may cause added burdens on marriage and family. Theresa and I discovered that leisurely walks is good therapy for communication and romantic discoveries displayed in nature's beauty.

6

Relaxation

Our beliefs and perceptions about life are not always true. They are only what we think, believe, and perceive. Learn to relax, visualize your goal and objective, and truly believe that you can take positive action to succeed in life. Learn to disable negative thoughts and feelings; they will weaken your belief system.

On my computer, I have protection against viruses. If I install certain programs, I have to disable the antivirus program to entertain the other program. Our minds work the same way. Our minds cannot perform to their full potential if negative thoughts impede the flow of positive energy, which rejuvenates spiritual belief in God's creative power. For example, if we do not believe that marriage is a lifetime commitment, we will experience an overload of negative emotions when we experience challenges in our relationship.

Many people experience far less than they desire in life because of negative perception and how they view the things around them. Others may experience harmonious, fulfilling, and truly wholesome lives—because they truly believe such lives are possible. If we *believe* that we will experience a rich, fulfilling married life, and we learn to relax and allow our minds to dwell on the quality things that a wife and husband need to apply to their lifestyle—such as learning to understand each other's needs, and making adjustments and allowances for the best outcome—we will have a successful, loving, caring, joyful marriage.

When we choose to follow the instruction God gave to the first married couple, our capacity to see things and achieve success will be well beyond what we think we can have. We will expand and enhance marriage and family beyond the boundaries of separation and divorce. When we choose to allow ourselves to do what is right for each other, we automatically enhance our capacities and our capabilities to imagine, conceive, think, and believe in more relaxed and balanced frames of mind. We experience real, loving family lifestyles that will take their rightful and meaningful places in the family environment.

When we think positively in our journey of life, we enhance our capability to achieve the goal of joyful living. When our beliefs and opinions become in tune with Christ's infinite will, we then enable our minds to relax and become the center for spiritual, mental, and emotional family values, and this supersedes the conventional overload and lifestyle stressors that are destroying marriage and family.

I choose to see the journey of life as an unerring and unwavering higher extension of a quality lifestyle that allows families to relax and enjoy balanced lives, filled with harmony and real love. The important areas of our lives need balance. Most of us do not allow valuable change to occur in our relationships with our families and others. We try to force the flow of energy. We want to get the most out of life without thinking of the cost. Many people destroy their marriages and lives because they want to be in the "express lane." They do not understand the capacity or capability of their limitations; they allow their beliefs, opinions, and perceptions to intoxicate their good judgment and wreck their marriages and families. Life, marriage, and family are precious commodities and should be highly valued. We can eliminate too much stress and transform our lives if we allow Christ's love and mercy to become our guiding light.

One thing that allows Theresa and me to continue our journey of life is the personal and ongoing transformation that occurs within our fifty-year relationship. In spending time and energy doing things together, we learn to understand and compromise with each other. Love is not selfish; love respects the value of patience, compassion, trust, and dedication.

In our fifty years of doing things together, we have discovered that our individual beliefs and opinions are vast and diverse. If we do not take time to value and reinforce God's unconditional love in our lives, the challenges of marriage and family, traveling on the highway of life, can become hazardous and prevent us from getting to our destination safely. It's the very reason why so many people consistently experience stress, fear, pain, limitation, and discord, while others consistently float through life, carefree, loving, content, prosperous, and harmoniously enjoying God's bountiful love and blessing.

I have found that the greatest deterrent to enhancing our results is to become overly stress. I also have discovered that too much stress is the single greatest challenge we face as families and in our marriages. Stress distorts our judgment, limits our capabilities, and most definitely lowers our abilities to be more creative in our thinking and activities. Stressing ourselves never gives our marriages and families a chance to succeed.

You can reverse stressful moments, however, by not allowing negative thinking. Refresh your mind with positive thoughts, such as, "The Lord is good, a strong hold in the day of trouble; and he knows those who trust in him" (Nahum 1:7 NKJV).

We have our own opinions of what stress is, but regardless of how we define it, stress influences our lives and lifestyles. Perhaps the most prevalent and detrimental result of stress is its impact on our health, both mental and physical. We need to pay special attention, because without our health, none of the other areas of life really matter. Mental and physical health is the foundation of real wealth, harmony, freedom, and the reality that is built upon the foundation of God's love and trust.

According to *New York Times* best-selling author and cellular biologist Bruce Lipton, PhD, stress is the cause of more than 90 percent of all illness and disease. It's also the cause of 90 percent of our limitations and perceived failures of marriages and families. Stress, combined with negative perception and fear, prevents many people from doing anything. The fear and pain become so intense that many people believe that no other choices are available.

Stress also keeps us from achieving what we desire, even when we are quite capable of achieving our goals in every area of our lives. Stress also destroys self-esteem and causes some people to become distrustful and disrespectful of others, which can result in failed marriages. In addition, if we do not respect ourselves, it is difficult to respect a spouse. Husband and wife must learn to respect and support each other. Do not suppress your spouse's creative ability to climb the success ladder. Learn to inspire each other.

When there is a challenge, work together as a team to get over the crisis. Uncontrolled fear, even when it has a realistic cause, can lead to anxiety and depression. Things will become better when you learn to relax, expect the best, and take action to make things better. Expecting the best will allow you to put your whole heart and mind into what you want to accomplish. Consider a husband who is under emotional stress because he is out of a job and bills are piling up. He needs a wife who encourages him and works with him wholeheartedly in developing a plan of action. Complacency and doubt will distort your ability to succeed and will create fear of the unknown. Your brain gives you the ability to think. Use it to eliminate negative perceptions and accelerate your drive into a positive mental gear to get over the difficult terrain. You will never know what you can accomplish until you design a plan. The neural network of the human mind is your mental computer, available for your use.

> When wife and husband practice relaxation and work harmoniously together, they will strengthen their relationship, eliminate stress, and energize their neural network to accomplish realistic goals and sustain joyful living. Financial stress is the subjective, unpleasant feeling that one is unable to meet financial demands, afforded the necessities of life, and have sufficient funds to make ends meet (e.g., have to reduce standard of living). It is the perception of the financial situation that is implicated in the negative outcomes we describe in this report. *(Department of Psychology, Carleton University 2004).*

In this day and age, most of us hope, wish, pray, and wait for something more, but we never take action to get it done. I suspect that most of us consistently receive far less than we want to achieve, which triggers frustration that could lead to depression. Consistently receiving less than we want can prove to be very stressful. Every family needs certain things, and in most instances, it takes the cooperation and support of family members to achieve those things.

Have you ever wondered why the things you desire never come through? Have you ever wondered why some people receive what they want, seemingly with very little effort, and they seldom become stressed? Yet others seem to consistently come up short and receive less than they truly desire, no matter what they do, how long they do it, or how hard they struggle to achieve their goals.

I have learned from experience that there is an easy way and a hard way to get to our destinations in life. The hard way has led me down many stressful and painful pathways. Many of the things I believed I needed to be successful were not necessary. The paths I walked created some enormous fears, which only served to intensify the stress and pain. These stressful and painful paths, in turn, intensified and fed my fears. To be a good husband, I realized that I needed to monitor my errors, encourage my strength, and notice when my family and I were ready for new challenges. Like new learners in a classroom, we should be receptive to new ideas and not be close-minded.

I've since discovered that I didn't have to walk those stressful and painful paths. I walked them because at one point—as it is with most people—I allowed myself to experience some very intense stress. Then I came to an eye-opening and life-transforming realization. After needlessly experiencing much fear, stress, pain, and struggle, I realized that "common knowledge" can only produce "common results." That's why real success, real harmony, real wealth, and real freedom are so uncommon. They are values that result from taking action to make meaningful changes, added to having a close relationship with Christ. Making him the central focus of your life, moment by moment, will allow you to remodel and redefine the neural network of your mind. Your marriage and family will benefit from the mental, spiritual, and emotional awakening of your mind. Your self-esteem will improve and cause revolutionary changes in your life, which will create awareness of unconditional love and will cement your marriage and family to the foundation of joyful living. When you face new problems, your renewed mind and body will be programmed to reconnect to Christ's electromagnetism of faith and belief in real joyful living, no matter what storm is blowing.

7

Value of Forgiveness

In this journey of life, your intentions and desires shape your future. When you create a positive perception about what you desire and visualize true values of joyful living, success will manifest itself. This is because you are preparing yourself and your life for the results you desire. Use affirmations to develop a forgiving spirit and successful marriage, such as:

- I feel alive and enjoy my relationship today.
- I look forward to a productive, loving, and caring family.
- I am grateful for a healthy mind and body to provide for my spouse and family.

"For we do not have a High Priest who cannot sympathize with our weaknesses; but was in all points tempted as we are, yet without sin" (Hebrews 4:15 NKJV). This is our message to our married friends and family: Let Christ's love touch your heart and regenerate kindness and compassion. His touch will heal your infirmities and give you the ability to forgive. He can heal your marriage and family issues in the way he healed the sick woman when she touched his garment. Press close to him and touch his garment in faith. Wife and husband should learn to forgive each other, and it will provide therapeutic healing to their minds and bodies.

The forgiving partner needs to earn the wife's or husband's trust by demonstrating the character of Christ. "Let this mind be in you, which was also in Christ Jesus" (Philippians 2:5 KJV). When you learn to forgive, you release yourself of mental and physical stressors that are dangerous for your health and well-being. Any situation that frustrates you, especially when you believe your spouse is to blame for your situation, is a potential trigger for anger, aggression, and abuse. Wife and husband should remember that challenges in life are not failures, because fear of failure has kept many families from living successful lives and achieving their greatest potential. Fear is related to anger and aggression and many unnecessary confrontations. Remember, "The Lord by wisdom founded the earth; by understanding he established the heavens; by his knowledge the depths were broken up and clouds drop down the dew" (Proverbs 3:19 NKJV). Trust in him and learn the recipe of forgiveness, and he will supply all your needs, present and future.

Most of us have been hurt by somebody at some point; it could be family members, friends, or church brothers or sisters. Your in-laws may have criticized your ability to take care of your family or your parenting abilities, or maybe your spouse violated your sacred trust. These actions could leave you with lasting feelings of anger, animosity, and resentment, but if you don't develop patience and a spirit of forgiveness, you could be the one who hurts most.

By accepting the willingness to forgive, you can intentionally embrace peace, gratitude, grace, and hope of a joyful and caring relationship. Think of exactly how love and mercy can lead you along the path of physical, spiritual, and emotional wellness. The acid test of forgiveness is when you can visit your offender in your mind and not entertain any form of animosity. You have relived yourself of stress and negative emotions that are harmful to your life.

Extending love and mercy is a choice to let go of animosity and ideas of vengeance and to recreate in your mind the hope of better things in your life and the life of your family. The action that once angered you might stay to remind you of the complication of life, but love and mercy will give you strength to concentrate on other, excellent, and meaningful things of life. I have learned from experience that love and mercy lead to feelings of understanding and compassion for others who have violated your goodness and trust. Forgiveness does not mean that you minimize a deviant act. You could forgive the person without forgiving the bad behavior or action. Forgiveness brings peace and confidence to assist you in going on with life, and it gives you the opportunity to experience joyful living.

In 2004 most people in the United States had married only once, with 58 percent of women and 54 percent of men (US Census Bureau 2004) still betrothed to their first spouses. Still, the ratio of divorcees to non divorcees has more than tripled since the 1950s, and the lifetime probability of a first marriage ending in divorce is close to 50 percent (Teachman, Tedrow, & Crowder 2000).

Letting go of grudges and resentment paves the pathway of life and opens the way for peace, contentment, and serenity. When you're injured or hurt by someone you love, you may be angry, saddened, or disappointed, but do not allow this anger to take root in your heart. Do not dwell on hurtful events or bad situations; they will deplete your energy. You might be eaten up by your own anger if you permit the sensation of animosity to crowd out feelings of love and mercy. If you do, you then will be left destitute—and mentally, spiritually, and emotionally homeless. In many instances, it is not what you eat that affects your health; it's what is eating you.

Ask yourself, what are the negative effects of holding anger? How does anger affect you if you accumulate and hold on to bitterness and take an unforgiving spirit into a new relationship? Your life could become so wrapped up in the wrong thinking that you will not delight in the present and will destroy your ability to enjoy life. You might end up being distressed or disheartened, blaming everyone for your problems. You might feel that your life lacks meaning or function or that you're at war with your spiritual beliefs and your connection with God. You may discourage useful connections with friends, God, and others.

If you persistently allow negative perceptions to crowd out positive and joyful thoughts from your mind, you could become enveloped by resentment and sensations of oppression and frustration, which could lead to depression.

Forgiveness is ability to do the following:

- Take into consideration the value of forgiveness and the virtue it contributes to your life and the relief it gives you from stressors.
- Think of how you've acted or reacted to mistakes or challenges and how they have impacted your life, positively or negatively.

Are you willing to sacrifice your health by allowing someone to control your actions? Forgiveness is a recipe for joyful living. Give yourself freedom to evolve mentally, spiritually, and emotionally. When you forgive, you release the control and energy an offending person had (or has) in your life. It allows you to share the gift of real love. You also will be able to use your creative ability to help others who are having difficulty with forgiveness.

As you release grudges and anger, you won't define yourself by the way in which you were offended or abused. You also will discover concerns of others. Forgiveness could redefine your perception of life and allow you to develop the ability to pardon an offending individual for an infraction or misdeed.

Peter asked Christ, "How many time should I forgive my brother? Is it seven times?" I believe Peter asked the wrong question. The question should have been, "Why should I forgive?" Why should I forgive someone who caused me to lose my job; someone who violated my sacred trust; a husband who physically and emotionally abused my daughter; someone who robbed me? The forgiveness to which Christ refers cannot be determined by number. Forgiveness is not mechanical; it is personal and real. There are three reasons why we should develop an attitude of forgiveness.

- We should forgive because Christ has forgiven us. The Bible says, "But God demonstrates his own love towards us, in that while we were still sinners, Christ died for us" (Romans 5:8 NKJV).
- We should forgive because Christ asked us to. "Jesus answered and said to him, 'If anyone loves me, he will keep my words: and my Father will love him, and we will come to him, and make our home with him'" (John 14:23 NKJV).
- We should forgive because it is the right thing to do. Forgiveness is more beneficial to the person who is willing to forgive and accept forgiveness. How a husband or wife deals with stress, disappointments, and frustration determines the essence of his or her personality and character. Anger may do more damage and more harm to our marriages and families and cause us to entertain negative emotion.

The Bible refers to forgiveness in two methods. The Lord instructs us to repent of our sins and find his forgiveness. He additionally instructs us to forgive those who anger or harm us. There are two marital hazards: wives and husbands have to eliminate or control their own anger, and they have to know how to handle their spouses' aggression against them. Sin is a heavy burden that is difficult to carry. It brings the tension and anguish that is destructive to our minds, bodies, and spirits. We experience danger because we disobey the instruction of Christ. Christ asked us to love our enemy and do well to those who seek to harm us. Think of your pressure cooker at home; when the pressure rises above its set pressure, the safety valve opens to release the excess pressure.

If the safety valve does not open, the vessel will explode and cause damage to you and your home. When we allow resentment and anger to build up in our systems, we are in danger of having mental or physical explosions. It brings remorse as we understand that as a result of our activities, we may have injured others and removed ourselves from obtaining the good things our God has promised and is ready to provide to us.

The Bible refers to love and mercy in two methods. We can get forgiveness for our faults when we are totally and honestly committed to forgiving others. Forgiveness due to Jesus Christ's love and affection relieves suffering, pain, and death. The Lord's love and mercy brings comfort, contentment, peace, and serenity. Forgiveness restores our confidence and belief in joyful living. Christ says. "Come now, and let us reason together, saith the Lord: though your sins be as scarlet, they shall be as white as snow; though they be red like crimson, they shall be as wool" (Isaiah 1:18 KJV).

We can experience this miracle in our lives when we learn the true meaning of forgiveness, whether we need to forgive someone or ask someone to forgive us of our mistakes. God is always pleading with us. He asked us to love others as we love ourselves. "Come to me all you who labor and are heavy laden, and I will give you rest. Take my yoke upon you and learn from me, for I am gentle and lowly in heart, and you will find rest for your souls. For my yoke is easy and my burden is light" (Matthew 11:28–30 NKJV). When you rid yourself of the offenses you have committed, you allow yourself to get a new heart and a new spirit. "Cast away from you all the transgression which you have committed, and get yourself a new heart and a new spirit. For why should you die, O house of Israel?" (Ezekiel 18:31 NKJV). In life, I have discovered that it is very easy to become angry and resentful when something goes wrong.

In such circumstances, learn to pray; be in tune with God's guidance. To be angry is not the Lord's direction. He demonstrated forgiveness when he was nailed to the cross. He asked that forgiveness be given to those who nailed him to the cross because they were ignorant and unlearned people who did not understand his mission of salvation. Stephen followed his example by asking forgiveness for those who stoned him. When we exercise forgiveness, we allow joyful messages to flow through our minds and allow our thoughts to entertain love for God and others.

You should pray for strength to forgive the spouse who has wronged you, and you must release feelings of vengeance, bitterness, or anger. Likewise, search for the good in your spouse instead of concentrating on his or her mistakes and multiplying his or her weaknesses. God will be the judge of anyone's abusive or unfaithful actions and indiscretions.

Selfishness brings suffering and discomfort; the Lord's love and mercy brings comfort, pleasure, and hope to our hearts. In addition to finding love and mercy for your mistakes, you will be motivated and eager to forgive selfish behavior. You may not have the option of reinstating your relationship with your husband or wife because that is out of your control. You can release your anger, however, and free yourself from emotional stress that will entertain animosity in your life and rob you of your blessings of peace, contentment, and joyful living.

I am not an advocate for staying in an abusive relationship. If you find yourself in such a situation, remember that God has given you a mind to think. Prayerfully use it, and make the right decision. God is love. He does not support mental, physical, or emotional abuse. Jesus maintained a perfect attitude in every situation because he prayed about everything. We too should seek God's guidance about every aspect of our lives and allow him to work out his perfect will within our lives. Jesus's attitude was never for us to become defensive or defenseless, discouraged, or depressed. His goal is for us to please him and others, rather than to achieve our own agendas. "Husbands, love your wives, even as Christ also loved the church and gave himself for it" (Ephesians 5:25 NKJV).

"Prayer unites us with one another and with God. Prayer brings Jesus to our side, and gives to the fainting, perplexed soul new strength to overcome the world, the flesh and the devil" (White 1941).

For those who are divorced and remarried, let Jesus be your guiding light. Do not worry about the past, and let Christ take care of the future. When cells become a part of tissue or organs, they lose the ability to work alone and cannot survive without the support of other cells. When a wife and a husband become one in marriage, it is difficult for either to function alone. They are no longer two but one in purpose and action. There is one important factor wife and husband always should keep in mind: be mindful of anger. An article in *Psychology Today* (1983) suggests that anger is related to violence, crime, and spouse and child abuse. Learn to control your anger and be willing to forgive each other, and you will be one in mind and body.

8

Value of Integrity

We may assume that all of our decisions will be personally fulfilling, and that our employers, coworkers, the government, and our communities will have our best interests at heart. In many instances, these assumptions are correct, but there are times when there is a total breakdown of our expectations. Our planning was not properly examined; our decisions were based on the assumption that everyone's integrity is the same. When this happens, if we are not emotionally prepared, our confidence could be broken and lead to unhealthy behavior that is destructive to our marriages and families.

Always allow integrity to have a strong foundation in Christ, so that you will consciously support your decision, regardless of the outcome. Sometimes you may assume that your decisions are correct, because your friends or organizations may influence you to believe that these are the right decisions. Your integrity depends on your own decisions, not the decisions of others. You may pick up unhealthy emotions from your environment, but if you do not develop the ability to release those unhealthy emotions, you could hurt your integrity and the integrity of your marriage and family.

Never assume that everything you are taught by family, friends, and community is correct. Be consciously aware of the pathway you choose to take in your real journey of life. People may have good intentions, but in life, you are responsible for your actions.

Sometimes, you may make bad decisions as you travel through life's challenging pathways. Learn to be a critical but positive thinker, because your life and your family depend on your integrity in a society and culture that emphasizes goal-oriented and task-driven behavior. If you are to integrate into this type of working community, integrity is an essential tool for supporting and building character.

Integrity always sets high standards and sticks to them. Choose words and actions that are sincere, and never try to mislead anyone. Stand up for what you believe in; do not follow the crowd. Your true character defines itself when you are under stress. Learn from your mistakes, as they will save you from failure. Success will come and go, but integrity stands forever. Integrity means doing the right thing at all times and in all circumstances, whether or not anyone is watching you. It takes courage and strength to do the right thing, no matter what the consequences will be. Most marriages and families are destroyed, because lack of integrity costs jobs and destroys reputations and joyful living.

Building a reputation of integrity takes a lifetime, but it takes only a second to lose. Never allow yourself to do anything that would damage your integrity. We live in a competitive world, where integrity loses its real value. Most people believe in survival of the fittest. Many people live by the philosophy that everything is all right—that it is okay to lie if you lie with a little finesse; that it's all right to cheat and steal if you are a dignified thief (so that it will not be called thievery but embezzlement); and that it's all right to cheat and deceive if you do it under the deception of love and compassion. This so-called philosophy is destroying the integrity of our society and family values.

At work, you may do just enough to get by. You cheat yourself with the perception that companies have lots of money—they can pay more, so why kill yourself? Cheating at work will lead to cheating at home. Honesty will improve your ability to take care of your marriage and family in challenging and difficult environments. Never overstate your qualifications because you want the highest evaluation possible from a prospective employer. Do not cover up your mistakes because you are afraid of getting fired; you will endanger your life and the lives of your friends and family. Everything you do in your journey of life affects your marriage and family and impacts joyful living.

Many people find perfectly valid reasons why they do things that destroy the integrity of their marriages and families. Dishonesty may provide instant gratification, but it won't last. If you want to be successful in life, build up your integrity with your family, work, and community.

Some people without integrity seem to be successful without ever getting caught. They create a false perception by wearing masks to cover their deception, but their success will last only for a time. Do not envy them. They are working under pressure, trying to play the game of superiority. These people could have gained the results they wanted if they had honestly taken the time and effort to work to achieve their goals. Instant gratification can come at a very high cost. Many people have ruined their integrity, their health, and their families to gain instant success. Real health and wealth is gained by building your integrity and the integrity of your marriage and family. Do not value your wealth by your material position. There is much more value to a balanced lifestyle when it sustains joyful living. When you have lost your ability to be trusted as a person of integrity, you have lost the most valuable quality of life.

Gaining power by false pretences results in the loss of your reputation; you will be permanently damaged. Christian virtue is nurtured by integrity and a loving relationship. The strength and the success of marriages and families depends on quality men and women who are willing to sacrifice personal power and gratification and who will work as a team to accomplish the goal of building marriages and family relationships that are free from negative incidents, deceit, and negative baggage. Remember: garbage in, garbage out—what you put in is what you take out. If you build your integrity on love and trust, you will earn love and trust that strengthen your marriage and family.

Husbands should take note of the following study, published by *Science Daily*:

> When it comes to a happy marriage, a new Rutger study finds that the more content the wife is with the long-term union, the happier the husband is with his life no matter how he feels about their nuptials.

> "I think it comes down to the fact that when a wife is satisfied with marriage she tends to do a lot more for her husband, which has a positive effect on his life," said Deborah Carr, a professor in the Department of Sociology, School of Arts and Science. "Men tend to be less vocal about their relationships and their level of marital unhappiness might not be translated to their wives. *(Science Daily 2014).*

"Give and it will be given to you. A good measure, pressed down, shaken together and running over, will be poured into your lap. For with the measure you use, it will be measured to you" (Luke 6:38 NIV).

When this goal is accomplished, everyone achieves real healthy and wealthy, loving, and caring relationships that last for a lifetime. Integrity empowers and builds your self-esteem. "Yet self-esteem is a fundamental human need. Its impact requires neither our understanding nor our consent. It works its way within us without our knowledge" *(Branden 1994).*

In my research, I discovered that marriages during the Renaissance were not personal matters; they were crucial to the network of alliances that elevated a family's prosperity and prestige, and they formed the fabric of loyalty, affection, and obligation that supported civic institutions. Arranging a suitable match involved family, friends, associates, and political allies. In most aristocratic families, marriages were financial arrangements; daughters were exchanged from father to husband. It was not much different among the merchant families—women were viewed as property and were passed from one owner to another (that is, from father to husband). In Florence, Italy, during the Renaissance, girls as young as fourteen were often married to men in their thirties, partly to ensure the bride's virginity.

So then, how do we value marriage? Does money influence marriage arrangements in our Western society? You be the judge. Wives, respect your husbands. Allow them to take their rightful places as heads of the family. Think of your son. How would you like your daughter-in-law to behave? Mothers, you are always protective of your sons. Remember that your husband is another mother's son. Husbands, love and respect your wives. You are setting examples for your sons and daughters. They are patterning your behavior. Men must take back their rightful place as responsible leader of their homes.

I am appealing to men that they be men and take responsibility for their actions. There are too many single mothers taking care of their children. Where are the fathers? Are real men becoming an endangered species? Men, stand up and let your voices be heard. Rebuild the ethical foundation of family values. When my son-in-law became engaged to my daughter, he gave us the following certificate of commitment.

CERTIFICATE OF ENGAGEMENT

This is to certify that on Thursday the twenty seventh day of August nineteen hundred and ninty-eight, I Kevin A Benta asked Caphelle A McLaren for her hand in marriage, and she has accepted.

With this certificate comes a promise to fulfill my main responsibility as a husband, it is found in Ephesians 5:25,28 and 29, which states:

25: Husbands love your wives, as Christ loved the Church, and gave himself for it.

28: So ought men to love their wives as their own bodies. He that loveth his wife loveth himself.

29: For no man ever yet hated his own flesh; but nourisheth and cherisheth it, even as the Lord the Church.

In God we trust

I have asked several people to define the value of their marriages and families. I received many interesting and encouraging answers. Three of those answers are as follows:

Lionel and Shirley Quanchan, married for fifty-seven years, stated that their commitment to each other is more important than physical or material enjoyment. They believe that marriage is an institution designed by God to allow two people to share their future together. As Christians, they also gave their commitment to God and their family. Their love does not change; in difficult times it brings them closer together.

Mr. and Mrs. Oswald Miller, married for over forty years, voiced similar words. I stayed at their home in Edmonton, Alberta, Canada, when I was working away from home. They have family worship each morning and evening. When they have a disagreement, they work with each other to solve it—without disrespecting each other's rights and opinions as individuals. They believe that the value of staying married is a God-given gift.

Ursula and Philbert Joshua were married for sixty-one years. They valued their vow, for better or for worse, until death parted them. When Philbert was critically ill, Ursula refused to place him in a nursing home. Although she had her own health issues, she devoted her time to be at his bedside daily. She was faithful to her pledge to keep him out of a nursing home until the day he passed away.

Theresa and I are inspired by these loving and caring families. Their devotion provides social values to us and our community and society.

9

Power of You

As you know by this point, Theresa and I are celebrating fifty years of a challenging journey of life together. As we reflect on our experiences, we realize that every moment has been precious; all have been learning experiences that provided rich rewards.

In sports, outstanding players and coaches are inducted into the Hall of Fame. We hope that marriages and family values will be inducted into the "Marriage and Family Hall of Fame." Many people have completed this journey. My wife and I feel joyful to join them in the "Marriage Hall of Fame." For us, the journey will continue until death or Christ's Second Coming.

In the pages of this book, I have used our experiences and analogy of the human body to convey messages of hope, love, and joyful assurance to those who are traveling on this challenging highway of life. In my seventy-four years, I have experienced many changes. When the children of Israel journeyed through the wilderness to the Promised Land, most of those who started on the journey viewed the land from the border, but they never reached it because of their doubt. I have learned that we are in command of our destinies, and the choices we make will determine our destinations. Remember the old saying, "Everything that glitters is not gold." When you choose your life partner, remember that beauty starts from within.

When I was in my teens, I saw many so-called beautiful young ladies and wished I could have one for my wife. In my adult years, I saw these same ladies, and I said, "Thank you, Lord, for helping me to choose my wife." As you reach the golden years of your life, physical features will change. Allow yourself to see these changes as evidence of precious years that your partner has devoted to you and shared with you; cherish them. My wife and I are fortunate to be alive to enjoy this time with our children, grandchildren, and great-grandchildren. We feel blessed. The Bible says, "The days of our years are threescore years and ten; and if by reason of strength they be fourscore years, yet is their strength labor and sorrow; for it is soon cut off, and we fly away" (Psalm 90:10 NKJV). By reason of strength, my wife and I are celebrating our fiftieth wedding anniversary and have the wonderful privilege of enjoying the relationship of our children, grandchildren, and great-grandchildren, together in love and harmony.

Christ's unconditional love is the motivational force that has generated and sustained our marriage on the highway of life. Love creates within us the capability and capacity to achieve joyful living and to motivate intuitiveness, creativity, and independence, as well as the flexibility to manage and adapt to technological changes. "Oh give thanks to the Lord, for he is good! For his mercy endures forever!" (Psalm 118:1 NKJV).

Theresa and I do not worry about old age; together, we find comfort in God's amazing grace. I have talked to seniors who have lost loved ones, who have been divorced, or who never have been married, and what they fear most in their final journey of life is loneliness. I worked in the oil and sand industry in Alberta. During my two weeks away from home, I talked with my wife on my cell phone every morning and on Skype every evening, but it was not the same as being at home. We enjoy each other's touch, tender loving care, and the companionship that binds us together.

I have searched for a clear definition of marriage, and I've come to the realization that there a missing link in our marriage system. The missing link is our spiritual connection with our Creator. In the journey of life, we are more than commuters who require physical transportation. We are souls, clothed in the divine power of God's love, mercy, and intimate affection. We are secured vessels, fashioned and crafted by our Creator to carry the spark of life and to illuminate the pathway of hope and assurance of joyful living. Without that spark of life, we are nothing more than a lifeless collection of elements.

It is within this spiritual connection that our journeys begin and end. The things we say and do, the material things we cherish, the air we breathe, and the food we eat should remind us that we are mortal, earthbound creatures in need of spiritual, physical, and emotional wholeness. To successfully enjoy our marriages and families, we need that special connection.

It is with this unique, elevated spiritual reasoning, wisdom, and knowledge that we will discover the ability to develop the full potential blessing of our Creator's love and mercy, which will ignite the spark of love that we need in difficult times. Theresa's and my fifty years together have taught us that anger and unforgiving attitudes are dangerous enemies to marriage, family, and health. These enemies will deplete energy and create emotional pain; they will create a physical, mental, and spiritual disease that will wear you down and defeat your effort and willingness to continue on your marital journey.

When you are struggling with decisions, take courage and remember you are not alone. Others are experiencing the same challenges. If you take the time to help others, you could help to bridge the gap of despair and provide a path for others to cross into the arms of safety. Seniors who are lonely and who worry about the future and the death of loved ones should take courage. Death is not a sentence of despair and agony; it is an open door to hope and eternal life.

"Two are better than one. Because they have a good reward for their labor. For if they fall, one will lift up his companion. But woe to him who is alone when he falls. For he has no one to help him up. Again, if two lie down together, they will keep warm; but how can one be warm alone?" (Ecclesiastes 4:9–11 NKJV).

You may try to convince yourself that you do not have any weaknesses. When you are conscious of your weaknesses, however, you will be in a better position to eliminate or control your negative perceptions. If you play the game of superiority, you will be the only one who is aware of the game. You will believe you are winning because there is no challenger. You may tell yourself how good you are—the best in everything you do—but you will never feel content. Why? Because you will always feel threatened by your wife or husband and others. You will always want to be at the head of the game, never allowing real communication with your spouse. This kind of action causes anxiety and tension, which leads to emotional stress that is destructive to marriages and families. In life, always believe that you need others and that they need you. United we stand; divided we fall. In every building or structure, the foundation is the most important feature. When the building is completed, however, you do not see the foundation; you see the beautiful structure—but without the foundation, the building would collapse. Your marriage and family need a solid foundation for the beauty to be seen by others.

Teamwork is the most important factor in every marriage and family, large or small. To succeed in life, always respect other people's opinions. If we were all created alike or we all thought alike, life would be boring and lead to dysfunctional families. Specifically, your life events, conditions, circumstances, and experiences would be limited and would lack foundation. The family environment is where the foundation of real healthy and wealthy marriage and family begins. It is my hope that this book will assist you in truly awakening your understanding of what you can experience when wives and husbands work together to secure their marriages and families.

There will be true transformation in your own life, which you made available and possible by choosing to elevate your power of real love and affection. Explore your conscious perception at a deeper level. Your conscious awareness of who you are is the real test in life's journey. Without being aware of your strengths and weaknesses, you will not give yourself the proper tools to function efficiently. Your conscious perception of the world will determine how you succeed in your journey of life. It is imperative that you become aware of the essential factors of life and the circumstances for success in marriage and family relationships. Discover how you can consciously improve your awareness of the things around you in your search for joyful living.

> "One grain of sand at a time. One task at a time." By repeating those words to myself over and over, I accomplished my tasks in a more efficient manner, and I did my work without the confused and jumbled feeling that had almost wrecked me on the battlefield. *(Carnegie 1984)*.

You must intentionally and purposefully develop an attitude of willingness to work and cooperate with your family. You must consciously choose to awaken your awareness of the challenging and hazardous conditions around you and begin to consciously use and empower your intelligence for the success of your marriage and family. You have the potential power to use it effectively. Use it in such a way that you harmonize your true talents to attain your goals, rather than accepting the things you do not want. In this environment where marriage and family are losing their value, you can awaken your consciousness to the success formula for a healthy and wealthy marriage and a joyful relationship. You will reclaim your power to make the right choices and take action to work safely and honestly with your family.

Never waver in assessing your environment for hazardous conditions that are threats to your marriage and family. There is no perfect plan in life. Use your time and talents to cooperate with your wife or husband to explore new ways to eliminate hazards. Make plans that will determine how every aspect of your life will unfold. Ask yourself, "How can I arrive at my destination in this journey of life?" Understand your potential and creative abilities to gain a healthy and wealthy life; it is within your power to choose. Trusting in God will eliminate negative energy. If you do not have the knowledge to choose for yourself, cooperate with others and work out a plan that is unique to you and your family. It may prove beneficial to explore new ideas and develop an understanding of cooperative effort.

Cooperating minds will provide you with a solid foundation and understanding of how and why unity plays such a major role in creating a successful marriage and family. The multimillion-dollar corporations that are successful establish boards of directors who work together to develop the best plan for the corporation to succeed. Conditions and circumstances in both your individual life and the life of your family depend on cooperation.

Creation determined how all things in the world around us came into existence to provide us with our basic needs.

Maslow's hierarchy of needs describes the basic needs that all human beings have, and it organizes those needs into five categories within the hierarchy. If the most basic need is not met, then Maslow's theory proposes that none of the needs higher up in the hierarchy can be met. The five categories of Maslow's hierarchy are organized as follows (from lowest level to highest level):

- Physiological: These needs are the most basic and are related to a person's survival—breathing, food, water, sleep, excretion, sex, clothing, and shelter. Without most of these things, a body cannot physically function.
- Safety: A person's safety can relate to several factors in his or her life, such as health, finances, and physical and emotional security.
- Love/belonging: These are the social needs, often seen as the need to belong, whether it is friendship, intimacy, or family.
- Esteem: Each person has a need to feel respected and have a sense of self-esteem. This is also maintained by feeling a sense of accomplishment or achievement.
- Self-Actualization: This describes a person's need to achieve what he believes he is meant to achieve. To meet this need is to reach one's potential. This need, unlike the others, can never be fully met, as it evolves as a person develops psychologically.

How does the hierarchy apply in marriage and family? Being aware of Maslow's hierarchy is in the best interests of both the husband and the wife. Wife and husband should use their knowledge of the hierarchy to structure their lifestyle and their family environment. Ideally, the husband would meet as many of the needs of the family as possible, especially safety. This, of course, assumes that the physiological needs of the family have been met beforehand. However, if the physiological needs have not been met, then the husband must understand that the family cannot work together safely. The husband would then need to make arrangements to help his family so that they are able to work together safely. Families are happiest and will work best if their basic needs are met.

Successful marriages and families provide value to our communities and the world. As wives and husbands develop programs and plans for their families, they learn to respect each other's ideas. You may have different backgrounds, which are unique. Wives and husbands should develop communication skills that set an example for their children.

The most important person for the success of any plan is you. You must take responsibility for your actions. Always reflect on your actions and attitudes and the way in which you relate to your wife or husband and others. Always follow the Golden Rule. "In everything, therefore, treat people the same way you want them to treat you, for this is the Law and the Prophets" (Matthew 7:12 NASB). It is vital to know what the rules for success are and how to go about following them. What are your goals and dreams for the future?

In life's journey, the things that you can see and experience in the physical world—as well as the unseen, in physical aspects of creation—can be traced back to God's omnipresence and control of the universe.

Visualize the aspects of your life that you wish to establish, and then develop self-awareness and be assured that with God, all things are possible. Consciously create in your mind the conditions and circumstances that make a real healthy and wealthy marriage and family life attainable, as well as experiencing God's bountiful blessings. Your true value will extend to your work environment and your community and will allow you to develop confidence in your ability to support your family. You will become accomplished in religious and other social gatherings and will experience a marriage and family life that is free from negative incidents.

The activity in which you are engaged every moment of the day is essential to the success of your marriage and family. Always master the tasks you are given every day. Positive action will empower you in developing an ability to assess your home, driving skills, work area, church gatherings, and social gatherings, so that you can develop plans to eliminate or control hazardous situations.

Your life is surrounded by hazards that constantly challenge your ability to succeed in your quest for a healthy and wealthy marriage and family life. It is important to develop trust in the people who surrounded you every day. Never entertain attitudes that are complaisant to working safely, because your wife's or husband's and family's happiness depends on you. There is a constant awakening of creative thinking in your mind. Do not suppress it. It is the potential power you need to unleash your ability to obtain a healthy and wealthy home and family. If you develop a method to perceive the best in everyone, you will experience the best in everyone, including yourself. It is imperative that you are conscious of your surroundings. Analyze and develop the best strategic plan to overcome difficult challenges, especially those that affect your marriage and family.

Learn to develop relationships—that is the key to creating the quality of life you desire. Your conscious mind is always exploring the things that are meaningful to you. If you feed your mind with rich, creative thoughts and love and compassion for others, you will develop a healthy self-esteem. Your conscious mind is what determines your awareness and the quality of a Christ-filled life. There is no greater barrier to success than the fear that you are undeserving of the things you wish to accomplish. In a changing environment, you need to be conscious of the health and safety of your family and social environment. Make a conscious decision to make Christ the focal center of your life.

My brother sent us a special gift for our golden wedding anniversary. I will share it with my readers.

> They say that two things you cannot hide are a cough and love. The cough usually is indicative of a cold, and love usually leads to marriage.
>
> But ah, marriage—what is it?
>
> Lots of funny anecdotes have been said about it.
>
> Here are a few:
>
> One man was asked, "What is marriage?" He retorted, "It's that thing when you get four rings; there's the engagement ring, then the wedding ring, and then come the boring and the suffering."
>
> When another was asked the same question, he replied, "Marriage is the chief cause of divorce."
>
> One boy asked his dad, "Father, is it true that in some parts of the world, a man doesn't know who his wife really is until after the wedding?" After some thought, the father replied, "It's the same thing in every country my son."
>
> Another boy asked, "Dad, how much does a wedding cost?" The father replied instinctively, "I don't know, son. I have been married for thirty years now, and I am still paying for it."

In Jamaica, one man was asked to define matrimony. Without hesitation and with a comical tone, he gave the definition: "Matrimony is when you get married, and you lose all your money after—even the money under the mattress. That's why it's called matrimony!"

These might be humorous, but the Bible has a different take on marriage. Hebrews 13:4 declares, "Marriage is honorable." As a matter of fact, the genesis of marriage is in the book Genesis. "Therefore shall a man leave his father and his mother, and shall cleave unto his wife: and they shall be one flesh" (Genesis 2:24). Marriage is an institution created by God during the Creation week. And whatever was created by God during the Creation week was meant for our unremitting health, happiness, and prosperity—an abiding state of physical, social, mental, and spiritual well-being. And the closer we get back to the garden of Eden—relative to nutrition, rest, marriage, and divine relationship—the better off we all will be.

Because of the entrance of sin in this world, marriage has become challenging, demanding, and even sometimes scary and frightening. For some, it is like a yoke of bondage. And no wonder! Most marriages are probably entered into prematurely or immaturely. Perhaps that is why over 30 percent of marriages end in divorce. Some of the reasons cited for this increasingly high rate of divorce include, incompatibility, infidelity, lack of trust and understanding, and financial strains.

With all this, how does a couple stay married for one year, or five years, or ten years, or fifty years?

I tip my hat to my bigger brother, Matthew McLaren, and his lovely wife, Theresa, for this milestone in their lives—their golden wedding anniversary.

I am sure they would be first to declare that it was not easy, that perhaps there were days when they felt like walking away from it all. But because they believe that marriage is for keeps—"'til death do us part"—they hung in there.

Because God created marriage, it must be beneficial for us. Consider some of the benefits of marriage: commitment; responsibility-sharing; companionship; emotional, social, and financial stability; a satisfying, guilt-free sex life with reduced health risks; and an inseparable bond with each other and God—among other things. No wonder Paul states that it is honorable for all and that the bed is undefiled (Hebrews 13:4).

We know that a fiftieth wedding anniversary is golden and a twenty-fifth anniversary is silver, but what if you survive just one year of marriage? After all, this is no ordinary feat in today's society. What symbol does one get? It is paper.

Why paper? Well, I guess it's because the couple is just starting to write their marriage history on a delicate scroll. Now they can discuss, determine, and document all their future goals and objectives.

A fifth wedding anniversary is symbolized by wood. This is when the marriage, like a tree, sends deep roots of strength into the matrimonial soil and branches out with fruit as well. I always believed that this is when a couple should begin to have children. By this time, they have had enough time together and have enjoyed each other without interruption. This is because when children come into the equation, the bonding dynamics change.

A tenth wedding anniversary is symbolized by tin. Tin is a preservative. The marriage has been preserved to this point. Now you have the preservative to facilitate its longevity.

A fifteenth wedding anniversary is symbolized by crystal. Now the marriage is taking on true value of sacrifice and investment and is transparent for all to see.

A twentieth wedding anniversary is symbolized by china. The marriage is now durable, of value, and long lasting but still has some fragility associated with it. Many marriages have been dissolved after twenty years. So even at this milestone, the marriage needs to be handled with care, attention, and vigilance.

To my brother and sister-in-law, again I say congratulations on your fiftieth, your golden wedding anniversary. I give you paper, wood, tin, crystal, china, silver, and every symbol in between. Take them all and place them in your golden bowl of matrimonial landmark.

May this book of experience be a blessing to all who read it, whether unwed, married, separated, or divorced.

—Earl McLaren, PD, RPh, 2014

In the Pro Football Hall of Fame, the inductees love to display their memorabilia. In our marriage and family marriage hall of fame, we should proudly display our souvenirs. My church's Family Life department gave us a plaque for our anniversary that reads: "Your marriage is a source of inspiration to us all, an example of a lifelong commitment that works. May you look back over your years together and remember the wonderful moments and best times you've known. We pray for God's continued blessing of love and happiness on you both. Congratulations. 50th Anniversary, February 12, 2014."

On February 13, 2014, we started a new chapter in our life together. It is our hope to continue our expedition to accumulate more marital experiences to share with our friends.

Conclusion

Marriage is a lifestyle that affects people's lives positively or negatively. The result depends on the individuals' attitudes and commitment to each other. To each husband—have you hugged your wife lately and told her how much you appreciate and love her? When was the last time you bought roses for your wife? Was it for her last birthday, or do you regularly surprise her with gifts of appreciation? I recently purchased a bouquet for my wife, and my mind reflected on the Sunday morning fifty-two years ago when I met Theresa. That encounter made a new start in my life.

It started as an ordinary day. It was a sunny, warm morning in Jamaica, the kind of sweaty day that makes some people moody and uncomfortable. I was heading on an ordinary mission, but as I stepped on to the city bus, everything changed. I was startled by the pleasant personality and electrifying smile of the young lady I encountered at the bus terminal. Her enthusiastic smile welcomed the warm day. I got on the bus, and the silent, friendly greeting that her smile shared with everyone on the bus must have warmed the hearts of a few sad and gloomy passengers.

It seems to me that some passengers were irritated by the heat; a few people grudgingly returned her infectious smile. But as the bus meandered through the winding street, a slow, rather magical transformation occurred when an insane man streaked down the busy, congested city street. The incident provided drama for our entertainment and encouraged a lively discussion on the passing scene. The incident was disturbing but an interesting exhibit of human behavior, providing a movie that opened our minds to some of the emotional lifestyles that exist in our social environment.

I delighted in the rich possibilities that Theresa's charming personality exuded; she offered hope to my lonely heart. By the time I got off the bus, I had shaken off the unpleasant feelings with which I had started the day. When she said, "So long. Have a great day," my heart gave a joyful response. The memory of that encounter has stayed with me for fifty-two years. I had just started working, but I paid little attention to my financial ability of taking on marital responsibility. My emotional enthusiasm on that day inspired a transformation in my life and gave me confidence for renewed possibilities and hope for the future.

My limited experience knew little or nothing of the challenging, emotional pathway on which a marriage lifestyle would take us. Yet imagine the good feelings that surged through my mind. As I contemplate the experience on the bus, I now realize that the encounter was a lifesaving peacemaker with energizing power; it helped me to bypass the irritability that clouded my mind and provided a new pathway to my heart. As I reflect on those pleasant moments, I am amazed at the lack of confidence displayed by some couples who contemplate marriage. In today's social environment, couples ask each other to sign prenuptial agreements before the wedding is arranged.

It is no surprise that the daily news is saturated with reports of the disintegration of social integrity and the safety of marriage and family. The onslaught of mean-spiritedness is destroying the sacred institution of marriage. This disturbing news saddens us and distorts our lives.

No marriage is insulated from this tidal wave of disruption and disappointment; it reaches into all our lives in one way or another. The last decade saw reports that indicated an emotional attitude of desperation and recklessness in our marriages, families, communities, and the world. Our lifestyles have taken on the social discontent that is surging through the lives of our present generation. "Health and happiness go hand in hand. Never has it been more important to understand the physical and spiritual laws of health than today when stress, mental illness heart disease … are ravishing our society. Is there a better way to live? Does God and nature itself process the secrets to long life and peace of mind?" *(White 1990).*

The twenty-first century charged in with a rippling rage of despair and discontent in the lonely lives of spouses and children—abandoned, neglected, abused, and entangled in the intimate web of marital violence and despair. This book is a guide to making sense of the senselessness that is defeating our commitment to marriage and family. As a Christian and, for the past fifty-one years, a husband, I have experience in the changes caused by irrational behavior. I am saddened by the trend of growing negative attitudes in our marriages and lifestyles. I hope that my passion and my encouraging people to entertain God's unconditional love in their marriages and family lives will offer healing therapy. Our present lifestyles are full of distractions. Husbands and wives need to take time to relax and meditate on things that are relevant to a successful spiritual relationship and reconnect with divine guidance. Husbands, think of how you can ignite enthusiastic, intimate smiles on the beautiful faces of your wives each day.

Let us go back to the garden of love, where wife and husband share the fragrance of joy, the velvet aura of peace, the essence of forbearance, the tender delight of kindness, the radiant beauty of goodness, the cooling wave of faithfulness, and the texture of gentleness and self-control that provides a refreshing, nurturing relationship of tender loving care. Love will always overcome evil. Good attitude will overshadow bad behavior. Kindness will erase selfishness. Faithfulness will ignite trust and confidence in our marriages and families.

In the last decade, despite the bad news, there have been some welcome and interesting studies in emotional behavior. Most dramatic are the glimpses of the brain at work. An article in the May 3, 2009, issue of *Health and Medicine* refers to breakthroughs in science that tell us that the brain can remodel (or rewire) itself. This finding provides hope for the future. Let us nurture and train our brains to actively move us into a positive mood of acceptance of others and allow our minds to visualize a joyful family life for our children and grandchildren.

Studies show us that the brain can create new neurons (neurogenesis). The brain also can change the structure of neurons throughout our lifetimes. I encourage you to study the application of the human mind and body. I have shown in previous chapters that cells and organs cooperate and work together to keep us alive and neurotransmitters provide harmonious balance and joyful emotion in the brain. The human mind and body are designed with five senses. We can train our brains to use our senses as avenues of communication with our spouses and our families; this will keep our marriages alive. Our senses can provide "marital neurogenesis" to rejuvenate our marriages and families throughout our lifetimes. Be diligent in everything you say and do. Every action or behavior sends silent messages to your loved ones.

Involve your mind with the intimacy of love. In the things you do and say to your family, make every word and action appreciative and appealing to their hearts. Husbands, when you are with your wives in public, do not allow your eyes to wander. Let your wives feel that they are the most attractive and beautiful ladies present. An affectionate touch will be appreciated and rewarded. Learn to use smell and taste in your lifestyle menus. Surprise your wife with the fragrance of intimate love and assurance. Wives, a man appreciates nourishing, tender loving care. Stimulate his taste buds and self-esteem, and you will be rewarded with the joyful marriage you truly deserve. Some marriages end in tragedy, but with careful and loving actions, by the grace of God, we can change bad behaviors.

We've seen married people with goals and objectives who worked, struggled, and prayed for successful marriages. But when the going got tough, they grew tired and discouraged and quit. In time, they discovered that had they persevered just a little longer, they would have found the joyful living they sought. Ask yourselves how you can develop an undefeatable attitude, one of the precious virtues in life. Never think of giving up, because if you do, you will talk yourself into giving up when you experience challenges. Some people gave up on their marriages and focused instead on expensive homes and entertaining lifestyles. In the end, they realized their decisions were wrong.

Theresa and I have celebrated our golden anniversary. Gold is a precious metal that is processed from rocks and other minerals and purified by heat. When you experience challenges, think of them as purification. "I counsel you to buy from me gold refined in the fire, that you may be rich; and white garments, that you may be clothed, that the shame of your nakedness may not be revealed; and anoint your eyes with eye salve, that you may see" (Revelation 3: 18 NKJV).

To stay married for fifty years, you must learn to develop patience, kindness, and an unselfish attitude. There may be times when we pray to (communicate with) God and ask for direction, but before he can give his answer, we hang up. With sad hearts, we realize we were not using kind, thoughtful words to our families. We were mean-spirited and selfish. We talked down to our loved ones and led ourselves into a quitting attitude. We forgot the promise to wait upon the Lord, that he will help us in times of trouble. "But they that wait upon the Lord shall renew their strength; they shall mount up with wings as eagles; they shall run, and not be weary; and they shall walk, and not faint" (Isaiah 40:31 KJV).

Begin your day by saying and thinking good, kind words—words nurtured with hope, belief, faith, kindness, and joy. Use powerful affirmation: "I can do all things through Christ." Act and think with and work on your sensory language. Try changing your negative words, and your whole personality will change. Reach for the good things in your marriage and family, and you will receive them. Take time from your busy schedule to relax. Let your mind seek peace and spiritual blessing. Exercising your thoughts can enhance your life. Include daily periods of prayer and meditation to relax your mind, revive your intellect, and reconnect with your family, friends, and social environment.

Read spiritual texts in quiet solitude in the morning to prepare you to face the challenges of a new day and clear your path. Spiritual visualization and meditation will strengthen your mind and bring peace and wisdom to guide your family. Be a student of divine wisdom. Seek the teachings of those who are wise in spiritual understanding and wisdom. The wisdom of God's words will save you from making wrong choices and save you from suffering. Take some quality time and go somewhere with your family to have an unobstructed view of real life in peace and solitude—somewhere elevated, where you can view the sunrise and sunset.

When I was a boy, I lived in the country. Our house was situated on a hill that faced the east. When I woke up in the early morning, before sunrise, I would watch the first rays of light as they illuminated the eastern sky as the day came to life. In the evening, I would follow the progression of the sun as it slowly disappeared in the horizon, displaying its rainbow of colors as the day came to its end. Those were some of the most pleasant times of my life. As adults, our lives are distracted from the beauty of nature by our busy activities. We do not take time to relax and meditate on the important things of life, such as our marriages and families. On our journey of life, we need to take time to read the book of nature, which paints exquisite pictures with eloquent words.

Good, positive words are medicine for your mind. Stay focused, and you will enjoy nature's abundant blessing. You will also leave a road map for others to use when they are planning their expeditions. Will you join us in a commitment to keep your marriage and family strong and durable by giving or recommending this book to your families and friends?

To Theresa, I say that you are the lily of the valley, the bright morning star. Continue to brighten the corner where you are. May your gracious presence provide comfort and joy to relatives, friends, and family as we continue our new voyage, our marital expedition in search of our future wedding anniversaries of emerald and diamond.

Bibliography

Andreasen, M. L. *Prayer.* Oakland, California: Pacific Press, 1957.

Branden, Nathaniel. *Six Pillars of Self-Esteem.* New York: Bantam Books, 1994.

Burns, Steve. *How to Survive Unbearable Stress.* Oxford, UK: Pergamon Press, 1990.

Carnegie, Dale. *How to Stop Worrying and Start Living.* New York: Simon & Schuster, 1984.

Chopra, Deepak, and Rudolph Tanzi. *Super Brain.* New York: Three Rivers Press, 2012.

Cohen, Barbara Janson, and Dena Lin Wood. *The Body in Health and Disease.* Philadelphia: Lippincott Williams & Wilkins, 2000.

Danes, Chuck. Enlightened Journey Enterprises. www.abundance-and-happiness.com.

Dossey, Larry. *Healing Words.* New York: Harper Collins, 1993.

Draves, William A. *How to Teach Adults.* Wisconsin: Learning Resources Network, 2007.

The Encyclopedic Atlas of the Human Body. Vancouver: Baincoast Books, 2004.

Goldberg, Linn, and Diane Elliot. *The Healing Power of Exercise.* New York: John Wiley & Sons, Inc. 2000.

Goodman, Eric, and Peter Park. *Foundation.* New York: Rodale Books, 2011.

Linder, Maria C. *Nutritional Biochemistry and Metabolism.* Connecticut: Simon & Schuster, 1991.

McLaren, Matthew E. *The Miracle of Love.* Mustang, Oklahoma: Tate Publishing & Enterprises, 2010.

Mercola, Joseph. http://fitness.mercola.com/sites/fitness/archive/2013/10/25/exercise-for-brain-health.aspx.

O'Toole, Marie T. *Miller-Keane Encyclopedia and Dictionary of Medicine, Nursing & Allied Health.* Philadelphia: Harcourt Brace, 1972.

Packer, Lester, and Carol Colman. *The Antioxidant Miracle.* New York: John Wiley & Sons, Inc., 1999.

Peale, Norman Vincent. *The Power of Positive Thinking.* New York: Prentice Hall, 1953.

Pert, Candace B. *Molecules of Emotion.* New York: Scribner, 1997.

Real, Terrence. *The New Rules of Marriage.* New York: Ballantine Books, 2007.

Rowland, David. *Endocrine Harmony.* Parry Sound, Ontario: Health Naturally Inc., 1997.

Runkel, Hal Edward, and Jenny Runkel. *ScreamFree Marriage.* New York: Random House, 2011.

Shostrom, L. Everett. *From Manipulator to Master.* New York: Bantam Books, 1983.

Siegel, Bernie. *101 Exercises for the Soul.* Navato, California: New World Library, 2005.

Sylwester Robert. *An Educator's Guide to the Human Brain.* Alexandria, VA: Association for Supervision Curriculum Development, 1995.

White, Ellen G. *Education.* Oakland, California: Pacific Press, 1952.

White, Ellen G. *Ministry of Healing.* Oakland, California: Pacific Press, 1942.

Endorsement

Dr. McLaren has eloquently expressed and shared the glue that has bound his affinity to his spouse of over fifty years. Throughout this volume, Matthew exposes his soul, and we are refreshed by the honesty of feelings, the integrity of his witness, and the fidelity that accompanied his half century of marital bliss. He has given us his "keys of success." Let's follow his lead!

Pastor Harold Johnson, master of divinity

Printed in the United States
By Bookmasters